READER AND SPECTATOR

A. Maria van Erp Taalman Kip

READER AND SPECTATOR

Problems in the Interpretation of Greek Tragedy

J.C. GIEBEN, PUBLISHER
AMSTERDAM 1990

CIP-DATA KONINKLIJKE BIBLIOTHEEK, DEN HAAG

Erp Taalman Kip, A. Maria van

Reader and spectator. Problems in the interpretation of Greek tragedy / A. Maria
van Erp Taalman Kip. -
Amsterdam : Gieben. - 149 p.
ISBN 90-5063-055-3
SISO klas-g 851.7 UDC 792.032.6
Subject heading: theatre ; history ; Greek antiquity.

CONTENTS

PREFACE

Each Attic tragedy was intended primarily for spectators who were watching the play for the first time and had not read it beforehand. This may be somewhat of a truism, but it entails certain consequences which in my view tend to be neglected. When discussing Greek tragedy scholars regularly comment on the original audience, on their response and their emotions. However, they seldom ask themselves what the audience were in a position to know and what they actually knew. What were the fixed elements of the myth upon which each play was built? Did the audience know these facts? And if they did, to what extent did this knowledge guide their expectations, enabling them to foresee what would follow? Is an interpretation based on information not yet available to the audience a valid one? Does it make sense to use the term 'dramatic irony', when the irony can only be perceived by a reader who knows the whole play, not by spectators who are watching it for the first time?

Most of the present study will be devoted to these and similar questions. I am aware that it is not always easy to reconstruct the knowledge of the audience, but I think it

1

worthwhile to at least make an effort. In any case, it is easier to reconstruct their knowledge than the nature of their feelings and opinions, which have been discussed by many a scholar with a great deal of confidence. In my final chapter I shall try to make it clear that this confidence is sometimes unwarranted.

My study will focus not only on passages from tragedy, but also on scholarly comment concerning these passages. This seemed to be the only way to illustrate the questions that occupied me, but it means that a certain amount of polemics is unavoidable. Otherwise, I might be accused of fighting an enemy who does not exist.

I wish to thank a number of people who helped me in different ways. Three colleagues read one or several drafts of my text: J.M. Bremer, W.J.H.F. Kegel and C.M.J. Sicking. I am very grateful for their suggestions and for their encouraging and critical interest. Miss L. Kegel assisted me during the first and the final stage of my work. As a classicist and an expert in the field of word processing she was of invaluable help. My thanks go also to Mrs. B.A. Fasting for her conscientious correction of the English text. I learned a great deal from her during our discussions. Finally I want to thank J.C. Gieben, who took over the publishing of this book following the sad death of B.R. Grüner.

1. READER AND SPECTATOR

In his book *Drama as Literature* Veltruský considers drama
exclusively as a literary genre, 'completely separated from
those components that are added in theatrical performance'
(8). In defence of his stand he argues that many plays are only
written to be read, and that many people read plays the same
way they read poetry and novels. Explicit stage directions are
'an integral part of the literary structure' (42), as they are
often redundant or impracticable on stage.

Veltruský's argument betrays a certain lack of historical
awareness. Drama may flourish in a society where most of the
citizens are illiterate or not in the habit of reading. And
though stage directions are sometimes redundant or impracticable,[1] this is mainly a phenomenon from the recent past. In
plays of earlier date stage directions are usually scant or
entirely absent, and in all probability they were not incorporated into the fifth- and fourth-century manuscripts that con-

---

1. G.B. Shaw even wrote whole scenes which, as he knew very well,
could not be staged. However, such jokes are not among the essential
features of the dramatic form.

3

tained the tragedies of Aeschylus, Sophocles and Euripides.[2] Thus no classical scholar would completely adhere to Veltruský's viewpoint, and few will deny that the plays of the Athenian dramatists were intended primarily for the spectators in the theatre of Dionysus. However, opinions are divided on the question of whether there was also a reading public of any significance and if so, whether the tragedians reckoned with those readers when composing their plays. It may be useful to discuss a number of the answers that have been given to this question.

I will consider first Vellacott and his book *Ironic Drama*. To Vellacott it is quite evident that plays were read: '...when the festival was over, the only element of the play that was available to the ordinary person for subsequent study was the text, more or less as we possess it today' (4-5). Leaving aside the question of whether the ordinary person *did* study the text after seeing the play performed, this is true enough. But Vellacott does not leave it at that. He holds that the meaning of the text, especially that of Euripides' plays, could not really be brought out on the stage: 'We must also acknowledge that it is difficult to understand how words spoken through a mask on the stage of a vast open-air theatre could convey the kind of subtlety we shall be studying - the innuendo of falseness beneath acceptable eloquence, the ironic pathos of nonsense spoken in good faith by an innocent victim. How could such subtleties possibly be perceived? The broad answer is that, in the theatre, they could not; but the complete answer must add

---

2. See Taplin 1977 (*Did Greek dramatists write stage instructions?*)

that, none the less, the subtleties are there in the text' (5). Finally Vellacott suggests that Euripides did not even want his subtleties to be perceived: 'A dramatist in submitting his play had to convince the board of selectors that it was worthy to be "granted a chorus", and in presenting it to win the applause of the populace. No unperformed play could survive. This helps us to see a possible reason why Euripides presented his most telling truths in ways which carried illumination to the sympathetic instructed spirit, and roused anger in the shrewd and suspicious reactionary; but which made it easy for the average obtuse listener or reader to be unaware that anything harsh or disturbing had been said' (19).

There is, to begin with, a certain contradiction in these statements. Vellacott assumes that few of the spectators were able to understand Euripides' plays. But if it were true that the subtle nuances of the text could not be brought out in the theatre, the only conclusion can be that *no single spectator*, however instructed and sympathetic his spirit, could grasp the meaning of the plays he saw performed. In that case we should have to accept that Euripides wrote closet-dramas and that the dramatic medium did not really suit him.

However, even apart from this contradiction, it is hardly conceivable that Euripides was hampered in such an unfortunate manner in his creative impulses and activities. According to Vellacott, Euripides considered Hellenic society 'corrupt and sick' (25), but unless he clothed this view in irony he would be unable to obtain a chorus. It was precisely because he clothed it in irony, that it remained concealed from most of his compatriots. Moreover, says Vellacott, even though the majority of the citizens were too obtuse to take offense, Euripides was always very unpopular.

It may be true that Euripides was not very popular, though even here there is room for doubt.[3] But the suggestion that Euripides, like a writer in some totalitarian state, acted as his own censor and consciously hid his 'message' in irony, is surely ill-founded. I also reject the idea that his tragedies were too subtle to be performed. Vellacott suggests that he, as a twentieth-century reader, is better equipped to understand Euripides' dramas than the fifth-century playgoers. However, it is a bit too convenient to base this argument on the masks and the open air setting of the theatre of Dionysus. Although we know a great deal about Athenian theatre practice, we shall never be able to fully reconstruct the interaction between performers and spectators. But if it were true that the actors were mainly intruders into the communication between the author's text and his audience, even if the author produced his play himself,[4] and if the actors were not able to act out an

---

3. According to Vellacott this unpopularity is evident in Aristophanes, but I find this view too one-sided. Despite his derision Aristophanes seems to have considered Euripides a foremost tragedian and the Athenians may well have shared this opinion. It is true that Euripides won few prizes; on the other hand, as Lefkowitz (103) remarks, 'the Athenians ... never denied Euripides a chorus'. Cf. Stevens, in particular 92-94.

4. This is indeed what Vellacott suggests. Cf. for instance: '...their contact with the poet was mediated by an actor and by all the circumstance of a vast gathering and a moving occasion; to us his words come direct from the page' (90). Or: 'The truth of Phaedra's position, and the Nurse's cry for pardon, were unlikely to reach more than a handful of those present; but the text was there for the reader' (235).

'innuendo of falseness' or to make perceptible 'the ironic pathos of nonsense spoken in good faith by an innocent victim', then there was no sense in staging plays, either for Euripides or for any other tragedian.

I now turn to Havelock who, in an extensive paper, argues that the considerable difference between the plays of Aeschylus and those of Euripides must be attributed to the growing literacy of the Athenians. He contends that the style and substance of Greek drama were closely bound up with what he calls a 'change in technology' (66).[5] Aeschylus wrote exclusively for listeners, while Euripides wrote for readers as well. Aeschylus had to write memorizable speech; for Euripides this was no longer strictly necessary. Aeschylus' central purpose was didactic; this purpose weakened 'as the culture came increasingly to rely on written forms of stored information available for re-use' (66). The Euripidean prologues are 'bookish', in contrast to those of Aeschylus. The fictional element, the unexpected and the invented play a far greater role in Euripides' dramas than in those of Aeschylus; this, too, Havelock relates to Athenian reading habits.

Havelock's argument raises many questions, only a few of which will be discussed here. On p. 92 he argues: 'We are not at the stage of true fiction in literature, and will not be for several centuries. But it is permissible to speculate that the

---

5. The term 'technology' is not quite satisfying since, as Havelock himself sets out, the art of writing was not of recent date. I also feel some hesitation about 'literacy'. Though literacy may have grown during the fifth century, it is probably not true that most members of Aeschylus' audience were illiterate. Cf. Turner, 9; Harvey, 628-630.

Euripidean conversations and lyric solos, so agile and typically
diversified, are directed towards listeners who are growing
used to reading, often in prose, what is no longer necessarily
familiar, that is, traditional, and therefore old-fashioned.'
Havelock does not explain what kind of prose he has in mind,
but he is probably thinking of sophistic treatises. But how
many Athenians really read such works? In all probability
only a small intellectual avant garde. Did Euripides intend his
plays for this small group? On the other hand, were the
dramas of Aeschylus traditional and familiar *in his own day*?
Havelock devotes a number of pages to the *Seven against
Thebes*; the other plays are, at best, only touched upon. But
does *Eumenides* not abound in new, unexpected and thrilling
events? One might even maintain that it is primarily 'fiction'.

There is some confusion in Havelock's discussion of reading and readers. On p. 66 he mentions 'that plays began to be
written with the expectation of being read'. Elsewhere he
contends that the spectators of Aristophanes' *Frogs* were
familiar with their tragedies because they had seen them
performed and had sung in choruses, *not* because they had
read them; they formed an 'audience of non-readers' (80).
Then again, when commenting on *Frogs* 1113-1114, he
remarks that 'the availability of readers in the audience is
recent' (89). These statements are difficult to reconcile.
Havelock apparently assumes that in 405 Aristophanes' audience *did* read books, but did *not* read tragedies. However, if
even the audience of *Frogs*, produced after the death of
Sophocles and Euripides, did not read tragedies, how then
could these tragedians ever expect that they would be read?

At the end of his paper Havelock once again mentions Euripides' prologues: 'As the century moves towards its close, the prologues of Euripides separate themselves bookishly from the action...' (112). Yet, this typical Euripidean prologue is already found in *Alcestis*, produced in 438, while according to Havelock the general literacy came about in the 'last third of the fifth century' (62). How then does one explain the fact that Euripides already wrote bookish prologues at a time when the era of the book had hardly begun? And if 'the change in technology' was indeed all-important, why did Sophocles *not* write bookish prologues?

Havelock repeatedly relates Aeschylus' style to the need for memorizing, but is Aeschylus' language in fact easier to memorize than that of Euripides? He points to repetitions in the prologue of Aeschylus' *Seven*, which serve to drive home the essential facts. But if we turn to *Bacchae*, one of Euripides' last tragedies, we encounter the same phenomenon. Twice during the prologue of this play Dionysus says that he is a god in human form, once at the beginning (v. 4) and again towards the end (v. 53-4). Apparently, Euripides wanted to be absolutely sure that his audience were well aware of this crucial fact. Readers could have checked the information by leafing through the pages - to put it anachronistically.

There is, of course, a considerable gap between Aeschylus and Euripides, but one wonders whether the difference between them was the *result* of the growing importance of books. I am inclined to think that the reverse is true. The same change in mentality that makes Euripides so different from Aeschylus also created the growing need for written texts and finally the 'tyranny' of the book, as Turner (23) puts it. I do not deny that, towards the end of the fifth century, the tragedians might expect their plays to be read by a group of interested people (cf. below), but Havelock does not succeed in proving that this fact essentially altered the way they wrote plays. If it did, it should be possible to show that, when he was composing *Ajax*, Sophocles did not reckon with a reading public, while in the case of *Philoctetes* he did. But Sophocles hardly appears in Havelock's paper.[6]

This brief survey of opinions would not be complete without the name of Wilamowitz, who was convinced that tragedies were read on a large scale. Since the plays were performed only once, the public needed the text of a tragedy for a better understanding of the piece. Moreover the poets could not really function as teachers of their people if their plays were not read by the citizens. Some decades after Wilamowitz published his view on the subject, Webster likewise emphasized the single performance: 'The Greek dramatist could only be certain of a single presentation of his tragedy on the stage, and therefore we may presume that he took steps to have his play published soon after its performance and to write a play which could be appreciated by readers, as well as spectators' (101).[7]

---

6. Havelock's remark on the *Oedipus Tyrannus* is completely incomprehensible to me: 'And yet also, competing against the factors of mnemonic control, one observes in the *Oedipus* the growth of architectural design, particularly in the placing of choruses between spaced intervals of dialogue, symptomatic, it is suggested, of the increasing intrusion of the reading eye upon the process of composition' (111-112).

7. Wilamowitz, *Einleitung*, 124; Webster, *An Introduction to Sophocles*, 101. In the second edition Webster left his text unaltered.

In a short paper entitled *The Single-Performance Fallacy*, Calder rightly protests that 'Mr. Webster's *therefore* is valid only with the acceptance of quite questionable assumptions' (238). Moreover, Webster forgets what Calder refers to as the 'straw-hat circuit'. Although it is probably true that no tragedian could be *sure* of more than one performance, the possibility was not precluded, even as early as the fifth century. It is generally assumed that at the lesser festivals in Attica old plays could be staged anew. There were regular performances in Ikarion and probably in Thorikos. We know from an inscription that Sophocles produced one or more plays in Eleusis, and Aelianus (*Var. Hist.* 2.13) tells us that Socrates went to the festival in Piraeus when Euripides was being performed.[8] Admittedly, the inscription does not provide the title of any play, and Aelianus does not make it clear whether, at Piraeus, Euripides was competing with new or old tragedies. On the other hand, there is no source which indicates that Aeschylus, Sophocles or Euripides ever produced a *new* play at a lesser Attic festival, and it is indeed highly improbable that they did. Why would a first rate tragedian have preferred such a festival to the much more prestigious Great Dionysia?[9] There is, however, one piece of evidence that seems to have been neglected thus far. Herodotus (6.21) relates how Phrynichus' Μιλήτου ἅλωσις reduced the audience to tears and how the Athenians, resenting this, fined

---

8. See Pickard-Cambridge, 45-49; 53.

9. Even at the Lenaea, which was apparently the second most important festival after the Dionysia, the great tragedians seem to have presented almost no new plays. Cf. Pickard-Cambridge, 41.

him a thousand drachmas. Moreover, they decided that 'nobody would be allowed to deal with that drama in the future'. Though the verb (χρᾶσθαι) is somewhat unusual in this connection, these words can only mean that restaging of the play elsewhere in Attica was forbidden.[10]

Moreover, the performance of Athenian tragedies was not confined to Attica only. Aeschylus produced his *Women of Aetna* at Syracuse. Euripides' *Archelaus* was clearly destined for the Macedonian stage, while his *Andromache*, according to the scholiast, was not staged in Athens.[11] It is true that there is only one actual reference to the *re*staging of a play outside of Attica: the performance of Aeschylus' *Persians* at Syracuse.[12] But there is perhaps some circumstantial evidence to support this.

At the end of the fifth century a large stone theatre was completed at Corinth. The need for such a theatre seems to imply that there was already a thriving theatrical tradition. Stanley (133) suggests that earlier performances took place in the *agora*. This may also have been the case in other towns,

---

10. The Greek word δρᾶμα cannot have another meaning than 'play', since τούτῳ τῷ δράματι refers to ποιήσαντι Φρυνίχῳ δρᾶμα Μιλήτου ἅλωσιν καὶ διδάξαντι in the first half of the sentence.

It does not really matter whether the story is true or not, since it would not have originated at all if no restaging ever took place.

11. Sch. *Andromache* 445. Though the scholiast may be mistaken, we cannot simply dismiss the possibility.

12. Sch. Aristophanes, *Frogs* 1028; *Vita Aeschyli* 16 (ed. Budé). Admittedly, the scholium is somewhat confused, mentioning two versions of the play. But it seems only natural for Aeschylus to have restaged a successful play when visiting Syracuse.

as it probably was in sixth-century Athens. Even in Ikarion and Eleusis no remains of a fifth-century theatre have been found, and yet we know for certain that even then tragedies were being performed there.[13] Regular performances apparently preceded the building of permanent theatres, and may have taken place at sites where no trace of a fifth-century theatre has ever been found. But if this was the case, then which plays were performed? Were there talented local writers who never achieved any fame in the outside world? Perhaps, but I think it more probable that Athenian tragedies, as early as the fifth century, were restaged, not only in Attica but also elsewhere in the Greek world, and by others as well as the author himself. War and politics may have hindered the 'export' of the Attic tragedy, but this need not have been a permanent obstacle.[14]

After this tentative suggestion, which is not intended as an argument in the discussion, I will now return to the 'reading theory' put forward by Wilamowitz and Webster. To support his view Wilamowitz calls Aristophanes to witness: 'Dass die Werke der Tragiker in den Händen des Publikums voraus-

---

13. See Dilke, 30-31; Biers-Boyd, 14; Whitehead 219 and n. 260; Stanley, 85.

14. If there is some truth in Plutarch's famous story about the Athenian captives, the Syracusans craved Euripides' poetry even in 413 (*Life of Nicias* 29.2-3; cf. Satyrus fr. 39, col. 19). It is noteworthy that Plutarch seems to suppose that the Syracusans' love for Euripides resulted neither from seeing his plays performed nor from reading them. He seems to think that they never knew any of his plays as a whole, but were only acquainted with random parts of his work recited to them, over the years, by Athenian visitors. I find this difficult to believe.

zusetzen sind, sagt ausdrücklich Aristophanes auch erst in den
Fröschen (1113), aber seine Polemik lehrt seit den Acharnern,
dass das Publikum so vollkommen mit den Werken der zeit-
genössischen Dichter vertraut ist, wie es nur die Lektüre
ermöglicht' (124). Webster employs a similar argument: 'And
if the Athenians neither read tragedy nor knew their tragedy,
plays like the *Frogs* would have fallen flat; only a small
proportion of the audience can have seen the dozen or so
plays of Aeschylus which Aristophanes quotes, since Aeschylus had been dead fifty years and it is hardly likely that all
these plays had been revived' (101). Furthermore Webster
refers to *Frogs* 52 and to certain passages in Aristotle.[15]
Since I am not the first to counter these arguments,[16] I shall
confine myself to a few remarks.

The passages from Aristotle referred to by Webster merely
prove that some people, among them Aristotle himself, read
tragedies. But even if Aristotle had informed us that the
reading of tragedies was the favourite pastime of every male
citizen of Athens, we would still be none the wiser, since we
are concerned here with reading habits in the fifth century, not
in the fourth. Vv. 52-53 of *Frogs* - which refer to Dionysus
reading *Andromeda* on ship-board - merely suggest that some
people owned and read scrolls containing the text of tragedies,
but are apparently meant as a joke. We may safely assume
that most spectators laughed heartily at the extravagant pur-
suits of the god. *Frogs* 1113 (or rather 1114), referred to by

---

15. *Poetics* 1453 b 6, 1462 a 12; *Rhetorics* 1413 b 12.

16. See in particular Sedgwick, Woodbury, Turner and Taplin, *Stagecraft*
15-18.

Wilamowitz, does not get us any further. Even scholars who take Aristophanes at his word quarrel about the kind of book meant here. There is, however, some risk involved in taking comedians at their word and Stanford is probably nearer the mark when he considers the line a 'gibe at the growing book-ishness of the Athenian public in the late 5th century'.[17]

However, the main argument in favour of a large reading public seems to be founded on Aristophanes' tragic parody, in particular in *Frogs*. This comedy met with such approval that it was staged again, probably at the same festival. While it may be true that, as is stated in the *hypothesis*, the play owed its success to the *parabasis*,[18] it is difficult to imagine the audience wanting to watch the whole play again if they found the second half a boring affair.[19] And if they liked the play as a whole, they must have known the work of Euripides and Aeschylus. But how?

As we have seen, Wilamowitz and Webster would say: by reading. Of the two Wilamowitz is somewhat more extreme, as he thinks that the Athenians could not even have enjoyed the parody on their contemporary Euripides, if they had not read his plays; Webster concentrates on the knowledge of Aeschylus' tragedies. Both, however, seem to imply that Aristophanes' parodies could only be relished by spectators

---

17. See his commentary ad loc. Compare Sicking 162 n. 2.

18. Weil's conjecture κατάβασιν must be rejected.

19. Sedgwick (8) supposes that, but for the *parabasis*, the play 'might have shared the fate of the first edition of the *Clouds*, which was placed third.' I disagree with him on this point.

who had read or seen all the tragedies he alludes to.[20] But if this were true, why then do *we* relish the parodies (as I believe we do)?

In the second half of *Frogs* Aristophanes alludes to or quotes from fifteen of Aeschylus' tragedies. In most cases the scholiast furnishes the titles of the plays, but only five of them are actually known to us, for the simple reason that the others have not survived. The same holds true for Euripides: we know only six tragedies out of 24 titles. To enjoy the parody it apparently suffices to know in a general way the peculiarities of the tragedians' style and composition. The Athenians could acquire this knowledge by seeing the plays performed and, as Sedgwick and Havelock suggest, by performing in some of the plays as members of the chorus.[21] It is true that only the septuagenarians were old enough to have witnessed any first performances of Aeschylus' tragedies, but thanks to the Athenians' honorary decree of 456, his plays could be restaged. The younger members of the audience must have seen such revivals of one or two trilogies perhaps, but not necessarily of all the plays Aristophanes refers to. It is also

---

20. Cf. recently, Knox (1985, 9), who argues that the scene beginning at v. 1119 'does seem to expect a reading knowledge of tragedy and certainly demonstrates it for Aristophanes himself'. Though I disagree with Knox about the 'reading knowledge' of the Athenians in general, he is undoubtedly right about Aristophanes. The tragedians must likewise have read the works of their forerunners.

21. Compare Taplin, *Stagecraft* 17.

possible that they had watched restagings at the rural Dionysia.[22]

Moreover, if it were true that most of Aristophanes' spectators were accustomed to reading tragedies, there must have been thousands of copies in circulation. Such numbers could only be reached if there were full-fledged publishing houses and a flourishing book trade. This, as Turner argues, is highly improbable: the book trade must have been 'a modest one' and it is very doubtful whether there were any publishing houses at all.[23] Webster's assumption that the dramatist 'took steps to have his play published' seems an anachronism.

And finally, even if the arguments drawn from Aristophanes' parodies were valid, they would only hold true for the last decade or two of the century and the last phase of great tragedy. *Frogs* was produced the year after the death of Sophocles and Euripides, but 50 years after the start of Euripides' career, 63 years after Sophocles' first victory and 67 years after the production of Aeschylus' *Persians*. Is one justified in ignoring such considerable differences in time, and in making such confident statements about 'the Greek dramatist', as if conditions remained unaltered during the fifth century? Likewise, when Webster (101) argues that Sophocles

---

22. Cf. Bulle (5), who stresses the importance of the rural Dionysia: '...denn aller Wahrscheinlichkeit nach waren s i e es, die durch häufige Wiederholung früherer Stücke die Vertrautheit mit den älteren Dichtern lebendig erhielten, wie sie uns in Aristophanes Fröschen so überraschend entgegentritt'.

23. Turner 20-21. He refers to Wilamowitz' theory as a 'brilliant and authoritative miss' (16). See also Van Groningen.

'must have considered his reading public', he forgets to ask whether such a public already existed at the time that Sophocles, some ten years after Aeschylus' *Oresteia*, composed his *Ajax*. There is no indication that this question should be answered in the affirmative. But again, if Sophocles did *not* consider his readers in the earlier phase of his career but did do so toward the end, it should be possible to demonstrate this by pointing to telling differences between *Ajax* and *Philoctetes*.[24]

It will be clear by now that I wholly agree with Taplin's opinion: '...there is no good reason to think that the reading of tragedy was at all widespread before the end of the century, let alone that tragedians composed with any consideration of a public of readers. ... No doubt tragedies were read by associates of the dramatist, by those who had for some reason failed to see the play, by tragedians, comedians, and rhetoricians who wished to use and draw on an earlier tragedy, by tragedy fanatics like Dionysus, and, probably above all, by those who wished to learn by heart parts of tragedies for private singing and recitation. ... But nowhere before Aristotle is there, so far as I know, any suggestion that the appreciation of tragedy by reading might be fuller or more developed...' (*Stagecraft*, 15-16). Some people did read tragedies - their number was small in Aeschylus' time, and increased some-

---

24. I shall not discuss here the views of Chancellor, who suggests that internal stage directions were meant for readers. To prove the existence of such readers, he simply repeats Wilamowitz' argument, without discussing any of the objections to that argument. Moreover, the examples he adduces from tragedy are singularly unconvincing.

what in the last decades of the century - but the tragedians composed their plays for spectators, not for readers.

It would, of course, be absurd to maintain that the meaning of a play or a single passage is restricted to what a first-time spectator makes of it. A work of art, be it a drama, a novel or a piece of music, never reveals itself completely on first acquaintance; our understanding can always be deepened. Thus we must take care not to dismiss a certain detail on the grounds that the spectator will not notice it, or to reject the importance of a verbal repetition because the spectator will not remember it. Such reasoning leads to arbitrariness. Moreover, the producer, whether this is the author or not, knows the whole play and knows it thoroughly. He may see to it that the detail is stressed or that the word that is going to be repeated receives particular emphasis.

In his book *Dynamics of Drama* Beckerman argues: 'We must remember, however, that the performers who communicate the action through their activity have already read the play. They shape their activity to accord with what is to come. In reading we have an incomparably more difficult task, to sense the action without knowing the future. That is why plays should not be read, but *reread*' (64). This is true, but though the actor knows what is to come and may give the spectator some sense of coming events, he plays a character who, as a rule, does *not* know what is going to happen. Despite the knowing producer and the knowing actors, the first time spectator has, during the earlier phases of the play, only limited information. Eventually he knows all, but by then the play is over. Thus when interpreting a passage from a play, the reader must try to regain the 'innocence of the spectator', or as Taplin has it: 'We should hesitate to explain anything earlier in the play in terms of something which is only divulged later, though we may reinterpret the earlier future' (*Stagecraft*, 18). Similarly Barrett says in his discussion of Euripides *Hippolytus* 490-2: 'But the first thing an editor has to do here is to *forget* what the Nurse is going to do, and to consider what the words will mean to an audience who have heard nothing later than these very lines.'

One more quotation to conclude. In 1972 Hirsch advocated adopting the following maxim: 'Unless there is a powerful overriding value in disregarding an author's intention (i.e. original meaning), we who interpret as a vocation should not disregard it.' (259) He considered this an ethical choice and though he did not discuss the intended public of the Athenian tragedians, I do think the same principle is at stake here. The consequences of this principle will form the main theme of the next three chapters.

2. FOREKNOWLEDGE

The reader, of course, cannot really regain the innocence of the spectator, nor can the editor of *Hippolytus* really forget what the Nurse is going to do. But they may at least try to determine how much information was available to the original audience. This is not always easy, since this information may have come not only from the play itself but also from the myth it was based upon. Scholars disagree on this subject; according to some it is highly doubtful whether the Athenian public did indeed know their mythology. I shall deal with this question first, as it is important to my argument.

It is a well-known fact that the evidence from antiquity is meagre and, what is worse, contradictory. On the one hand there is the famous fragment of the comedian Antiphanes, in which tragedy is considered a blessed genre, since the spectators know the story before a single word has been spoken. Tragedians need not explain things: 'I need only say Oedipus, and immediately they know everything else: that his father is Laius, and his mother Iocasta, who his daughters are and his sons, what he will suffer and what he has done. If someone mentions Alcmaeon, he has also mentioned his children, and told us that he went mad and killed his mother...'.[1] On the other hand Aristotle assures the tragedians: 'One need not therefore endeavour invariably to keep to the traditional stories, with which our tragedies deal. Indeed, it would be absurd to do that, seeing that the familiar themes are familiar only to a few...'.[2]

Not all scholars give equal credence to these testimonies. Kirkwood (252 n. 11), for instance, is inclined to believe Aristotle, while Lucas has his doubts: 'this statement can hardly be taken at its face value. In view of the familiarity with poetry which resulted from ordinary Greek education, and the familiarity with tragedy which must have been general if the Theatre of Dionysus was normally full at Dionysia and Lenaea, it is incredible that the great stories should not still have been well known' (ad loc., 123). He also considers it improbable that things had changed that much since Antiphanes wrote his *Poiesis*. Again, Else (318-19) does accept Aristotle's remark 'at face value', though he does not think it holds good for earlier generations and perhaps not even for Aristotle's older contemporaries. In his opinion the knowledge of mythology gradually diminished 'as the educational diet shifted little by little from poetry to rhetoric'. Moreover, tragedy itself no longer fed this knowledge, since the tragedians tended to concentrate more and more on the stories of

---

1. Fr. 191 Kock; Edmonds. My translation is based on the text of Kock. The comedy was called *Poiesis*.

2. *Poetics* 1451 b 23-26. Translation W. Hamilton Fyfe (Loeb Classical Library).

a few houses. According to Else, Antiphanes 'is exaggerating his troubles for comic effect, and it is to be noticed that as examples he cites two of the very best-known heroes: they happen, in fact, to be exactly the two who lead off Aristotle's short list, 1453 a 20 ff.' (n. 62).

Else's argument does not really succeed in bridging the gap between the comedian and the philosopher, as it does not explain why even the best-known stories were familiar to only a few people. It may explain why the knowledge of mythology had decreased, but if the range of tragic subjects had indeed narrowed, one would expect those stories that were chosen again and again to be common property. Antiphanes' praise of tragedy seems to confirm this. No doubt he is exaggerating, as one might expect a comedian to do. But his joke would be pointless if there were not some truth in it, and if even the story of Oedipus were quite unknown to most people in the audience. And yet, Aristotle seems to suggest that most people did *not* know about Oedipus. For what else can he mean by 'the familiar themes', τὰ γνώριμα, than famous stories like these?

Perhaps we must allow for the possibility that Aristotle, although not a comedian, is also exaggerating a bit. The prior knowledge of the audience is not the subject of his argument and his comment on it is merely a passing remark. At any rate, Else correctly observes that Aristotle is commenting on the audience of his own time, and Lucas' main argument, which is quoted above, no doubt holds good for the fifth century. Winnington-Ingram (1969, 132) estimates that 'a middle-aged man in the audience of Euripides might well have seen two hundred or more (tragedies), in which familiar stories had been treated again and again'. I would add that this same man might also have attended the performance of some 400 dithyrambs, many recitals from Homer, and probably from other epic poetry as well.[3] Even if he had missed half of the festivals and was not particularly interested, he could hardly avoid picking up some general knowledge of mythology.

This constitutes the external evidence, but we need not leave it at that. There is also evidence to be found in the plays themselves, evidence which it is possible to unearth by imagining a spectator who really knows nothing at all. I shall illustrate this by means of a few examples.

Towards the end of Aeschylus' *Agamemnon* Aegisthus unburdens his soul, recalling the horrible thing that Atreus did to his father. Much earlier in the play the murdered children of Thyestes have already figured prominently in the visions of Cassandra, but the seer does not tell an orderly tale and the spectator will not grasp the meaning of her words unless he already knows the story. Of course, he will understand that children were murdered by kinsmen (vv. 1090-2; 1219), but he cannot deduce from Cassandra's words the crucial fact that the crime was committed by Agamemnon's father and that the victims were the children of his father's brother. He may even think that the man who ate the children's flesh was also their murderer. At v. 1242 he is informed that the father's name is

---

3. As far as I know, there are no explicit testimonies about recitals from the epic cycle. I suspect that, as early as the 5th century, these poems were far less popular than the *Iliad* and the *Odyssey*, but I find it difficult to believe that they were altogether neglected.

Thyestes, but it is only in v. 1502 that Atreus is named, and described by Clytaemnestra as 'the cruel feaster'. By then an unknowing audience may guess that Atreus killed the children and offered their flesh to Thyestes.[4]

I admit that my imaginary spectator will gather enough information from Cassandra's words to understand that there is something rotten in Agamemnon's house and that his race is burdened with some sort of curse. But he will be temporarily at a loss to know the exact nature of the crime and the identity of victim and culprit. And it is difficult to see the sense of such a mystification, which would surely distract the spectator's attention, and force him to wait some 500 lines until he could grasp the entire meaning of the seer's vision. Thus, while the story of Thyestes' meal is not known to us from earlier sources, I am quite convinced that Aeschylus' audience were acquainted with it, and that Aeschylus appealed to this knowledge.

We turn now to the house of the Labdacids. When Sophocles wrote his *Oedipus Tyrannus*, the story of Oedipus had already been dealt with in the *Odyssey* and the Theban epics, as well as in a poem of Stesichorus (partly preserved on the so-called Lille papyrus) and in Aeschylus' Theban trilogy.[5] Though details seem to have varied widely, a few basic facts

---

4. It is not clear until v. 1585 that Atreus and Thyestes were brothers, and there is one detail in Cassandra's evocation of the past that even Aegisthus does not explain. Which brother violated his brother's bed (1193) and how was this adultery connected with the murder of the children?

5. This list is not complete. See Kamerbeek (1967), 1-7.

were always the same: Oedipus killed his father, king of Thebes, and married his mother, the king's widow, but he did so unwittingly. It is generally assumed that Sophocles's audience knew these facts and indeed it is hardly credible that they did not. And yet, Kirkwood, following the lead of Aristotle, is in serious doubt: '...one hesitates to rely much on the assumption of prior knowledge' (252 n. 11).

Here again I think that internal evidence provides the solution. This evidence is not furnished by the *Oedipus* itself. A spectator who knows nothing about Oedipus will respond to the tragedy quite differently from the knowing spectator, but he will understand it all the same.[6] However, an unknowing spectator attending the performance of *Antigone* must have been very much in the dark.

At the very beginning of the play Antigone mentions 'the ills derived from Oedipus'. She does not explain this reference and the unknowing spectator has to wait till Ismene elaborates on these ills (vv. 49-52). But what is he to make of these words? He may surmise that the girl's father was the same Oedipus Antigone referred to, and that he was a criminal or a madman or both. Ismene proceeds with the words 'mother and wife' (v. 53), referring to Iocasta, both mother and wife to Oedipus, but no one will understand this unless he knows the basic facts of the story. Without this knowledge one can only guess that the father's wife, who was the girl's mother, committed suicide because of her husband's death.

---

6. Compare chapter 4, where I shall discuss this difference at some length.

Kamerbeek comments on ἔπειτα (v. 53): 'not temporal, but introducing the second item of the threefold calamities (cf. τρίτον δ' (55). It would be perverse to assume that Sophocles here followed a version in which Oedipus' death preceded Iocasta's'. He is undoubtedly right, but this cannot be deduced from the text; it is clearly something we are supposed to know.

We take our own foreknowledge so much for granted that we rely on it without even realizing it. A telling example is v. 14, where Ismene says that the brothers died διπλῇ χερί. No critic or commentator is in any doubt about the meaning of these words, since it is common knowledge that Eteocles and Polynices killed each other. But the words themselves admit of another interpretation, as is clear from Jebb's comparison with *Electra* 206: 'θανάτους...διδύμαιν χεροῖν, a murder done by two right hands (that of Clytaemnestra and that of Aegisthus)'. The brothers might as well have been killed by two murderers or two adversaries in battle. The spectator who does not know about the mutual killing cannot really understand what Ismene is saying, and the mentioning of the Argive host (v. 15) does little to help him. Did those Argives kill the brothers and were they routed afterwards? And why, he will then wonder, does Creon forbid Polynices to be buried?

Admittedly, the riddles will be partially solved as the action proceeds. The unknowing spectator will learn from vv. 864-5 that Antigone's father was her mother's son, but he will never know that the incest was committed unwittingly, and will never understand why Oedipus, despite his sins, was once the revered king of Thebes (v. 167). He will learn from vv. 56-7 that the brothers killed each other and from the parodos that Polynices was general of the Argive host. He may approximately reconstruct the prior course of events, but he will again be at a loss when Antigone bewails her brother's marriage (869-71). Which brother of the two? And what did this marriage have to do with Antigone's death?

The prologue of *Antigone* seems to offer sufficient proof that the audience did know the story of Oedipus and of his sons. If not, one would have to assume that Sophocles saddled his public with senseless riddles, which merely hampered their understanding and could not fail to distract them from what is going on between Antigone and Ismene. But I have no doubt that he did in fact appeal to the spectators' prior knowledge. He had to make it clear from the outset that the girls who enter from the palace are Oedipus' children and that the brothers have just died. But there was no need for him to explain exactly what happened to Oedipus and his sons. He could confine himself to allusions, too vague for spectators who did not know the tale, but perfectly clear to a knowing audience.

I will conclude with an example from Euripides, again concerning Cassandra. After her raving, ecstatic wedding-song in *Trojan Women* she assures Hecabe that she will kill Agamemnon and destroy his house (vv. 356-60). In the following lines she alludes to the axe that will hit her own neck and that of others and to 'mother-murdering struggles'. Hecabe, who does not understand, does not believe her, and neither do the chorus and Talthybius: they think that Cassandra is deranged. But what about the spectator? If he has no prior knowledge, he will not know what to make of this scene. Though

Cassandra seems to be a seer, nobody on the stage takes her prophecies seriously. Why not? The spectator may well decide that the other characters are mistaken and that Cassandra's prophecies will come true. But how will this come about? Will she kill Agamemnon and be killed herself in revenge? And if so, who are the others who are to be killed along with her, and how does this bring a man to kill his mother? The tragedy itself provides no answer.

In his commentary on *Trojan Women* Lee appears convinced that the spectators possessed prior knowledge[7] and this was certainly the case. The whole episode only makes sense if the audience knows and understands what the characters do not, namely, that 'I shall kill him' means 'he will be killed by his wife because he brings me home as his mistress'; that the wife will be killed by her son in revenge; that Cassandra is a true seer and that she has been condemned to terrible isolation, since even now no one believes her; and finally that even the general of the Greeks will be a victim of this war.

In my opinion the examples quoted above are ample proof that the well-known stories were known to all, or at any rate most Athenians. They must have known the main facts about the houses of Atreus and Labdacus; they must have known the central myths surrounding the Trojan war. But we must be careful not to generalize. In his book *Ambiguity in Greek Literature* Stanford says confidently: '...it must be remembered that in a Greek tragedy Zeus, the author and the audience are generally omniscient in all the chief events that have been,

---

7. 'The audience needs only to be reminded of a story with which it is familiar' (135, ad 361).

are, and are about to be when the play is happening' (137). However, things are not that simple, as Stanford himself later admitted.[8]

In my first chapter I mentioned Aeschylus' *Eumenides* as an example of an invented plot. The spectators may have suspected that the protection of Apollo would save Orestes, but outside of that everything was probably new to them. Another example is Sophocles' *Antigone*. Antiphanes implies that in his day the daughters of Oedipus were as well-known as his sons. However, we may assume that it was Sophocles who *made* them known and that, at the first performance of his play, the story was new and surprising to the audience.[9] Likewise, the tale of Orestes, who brings his sister back from the land of the Taurians, while later quite well-known, was probably surprising when it was first introduced on the stage.[10]

There is one last consideration. It has often been observed that the content of myth was floating. If the tragedian based his plot on a well-known myth, there were only a few unvarying facts he could not ignore. Agamemnon had to be murdered by his wife and her lover and they, in turn, by Orestes. Oedipus had to kill his father and marry his mother and his sons had to kill each other. But everything outside these fundamental facts could be varied; the tragedians could

---

8. *Enemies of Poetry*, 133.

9. Compare chapter 4, pp. 79-80.

10. It is debatable whether Sophocles' *Chryses* already dealt with the story. If not, Euripides was probably the first who used it as the basis of a play. See Platnauer, xii-xiii.

fill out all major and minor details according to their wish. Only in this way was it possible that one story - like the Oedipus myth - generated a number of plays, each with a new plot and a new meaning. Thus, the audience had to use their prior knowledge judiciously. They had to call on their knowledge of the established facts of myth when the tragedian appealed to it. On the other hand, they had to ignore for the moment the details they might remember from prior tragedies or poems on the same subject. We shall now look at two examples.

According to the *Cypria*[11] Artemis demanded the sacrifice of Iphigenia because Agamemnon had shot a stag and boasted that, as a hunter, he surpassed even Artemis. In his *Agamemnon*, Aeschylus does not refer to this story and it is not difficult to see why. If Agamemnon had offended the goddess, this offense would in any case have to be avenged. And if this were presented as the reason for Artemis' demand - a reason which was in no way connected with the moral issues of the play - this would only obscure the dilemma facing Agamemnon: the choice between the life of his daughter and the war. Thus it is incorrect to assume, as some scholars have done, that Aeschylus expected his audience to fill in the well-known story of the stag.[12] On the contrary, the poet must have been sure that the spectators would *not* fill in the story. Otherwise

---

11. O.C.T. Homer V, 104.

12. Cf. Fraenkel, II 97: 'It is of no avail to have recourse to the excuse urged by Blomfield and others that Aeschylus did not need to explain the cause of the anger of Artemis since the audience was perfectly familiar with that detail of a well-known story.'

he would have found it extremely difficult to imbue the sacrifice with the meaning he wanted to convey; in effect he would have become the prisoner of previous poetry.

My second example concerns Apollo's oracle given to Laius as presented in Sophocles' *Oedipus Tyrannus* (vv. 711-14). This oracle has often been compared with its Aeschylean counterpart in *Seven* 745-51. In Aeschylus' tragedy the chorus relate how Laius was told by the god, not once but three times, that he must die childless if he wanted to save his city; nevertheless he fathered a child, overcome by his ἀβουλία. In Sophocles' play Iocasta does *not* say that Laius was warned; Apollo simply told him that he would be killed by his future son.[13] Most scholars consider this a telling difference. Aeschylus makes Laius responsible, so that Oedipus is a victim of his father's offense, while Sophocles does not.

However, Lloyd-Jones (1971) concurs with Perrotta in not believing there is a difference. He maintains that in Aeschylus' tragedy Laius' abduction of Chrysippus was the primary sin. It was because of this sin that Laius had to die without progeny and, when he again lost control of himself, he and his race were severely punished. Sophocles, according to Lloyd-Jones, implies what Aeschylus made explicit. There was no need for him to fully inform his audience, as he could trust them to supply the information which he withheld.

---

13. Kamerbeek (1967), 8, Kitto, 202 and Winnington-Ingram (1980), 205 n. 4, point out that the wording admits of the possibility that the child was already conceived at the time of the delivery of the oracle.

Lloyd-Jones reasons as follows. First he states: 'According to the Chorus of the *Seven Against Thebes*, Apollo forbade Laius to have issue, warning him that if he disobeyed his son would kill him and marry Iocaste' (119). Next he stipulates that, in Sophocles, Iocasta only mentions the killing, but omits the marrying, and thus 'it is hardly surprising that she should omit another (detail) which is not important for her purpose, that Apollo did not merely predict that Laius would perish at his son's hands, but warned him not to beget a son who would be sure to kill him. ... it is not true that Sophocles altered the form of the oracle' (119-120).[14]

Unfortunately, this argument is based on a misrepresentation of Aeschylus' text, since, according to the chorus of the *Seven*, Apollo mentioned neither the killing nor the marrying, but only the safety of the town. This version of the oracle is, as far as we know, unique. Aeschylus may have borrowed it from an older source - now unknown to us - but he may have invented it equally well. In any case, he clearly chose it because it fitted in with his interpretation of the myth. If Laius, by fathering a child, risked only his own life, his disobedience would hardly be serious enough to explain the fate of his progeny. But in Aeschylus' version the safety of Thebes depends on his temperance.[15]

---

14. Lloyd-Jones is arguing here against Dodds, who uses the same words but without negation: 'that is why he altered the form of the oracle'.

15. Groeneboom (ad 746-749) suggests another meaning of the oracle: If you father a son, not you but someone else (Eteocles) will save the city. However, this very strained explanation did not meet with belief. Hutchinson (xxviii-xxix) points out the possibility that in the *Laius* the

It makes no sense to say that Sophocles did or did not alter 'the' form of the oracle, since such a form did not exist. The oracle given to Laius was a fixed part of the myth, since without such an oracle Oedipus would not have been exposed. But the exact content and the circumstances around it were clearly among the details which varied. I agree with Lloyd-Jones that 'a tragedian may presuppose in his audience a knowledge of a myth which is indicated only by a hint' (123). However, this is irrelevant to this case, since we are not concerned here with knowledge of a myth. Aeschylus' version of the story cannot be equated with 'the' story.[16]

---

contents of the oracle were presented in a different way. I agree this is possible but I cannot imagine that in this play the safety of the town did not figure at all in Apollo's warning.

16.   Lloyd-Jones seems, moreover, to assume that all members of Sophocles' audience were acquainted with Aeschylus' Labdacid trilogy. But it must be remembered that, in all probability, *Oedipus* and the *Seven* were produced some 35 or 40 years apart. Unless the trilogy had been reproduced in the meantime - at the Dionysia or perhaps at some rural festival - only the senior members of the audience would be familiar with it. This same objection may be raised with regard to Saïd's argument in her article on Euripides' *Phoenician Women*. On p. 526 she concludes: 'Les *Phéniciennes* ne ressemblent pas aux *Sept contre Thèbes* ni à *Antigone* ou à *Oedipe Roi*. Mais il est clair que jusque dans le moindre détail, elles ne se comprennent que par rapport à ces œuvres, aux attentes qu'elles faisaient naître et qu'Euripide s'est plu à décevoir'. On p. 522 she mentions 'les attentes des spectateurs (ou des lecteurs) de Sophocle' but she does not seem to be aware of any problem here.

Only the septuagenarians in the audience of the *Phoenician Women* could have watched, at the age of twelve, the first performance of Aeschylus' tragedy and many spectators must have been too young to have watched even the *Oedipus* and the *Antigone*. As I maintained in chapter 1, a large-scale reading public probably did not exist. We may, here again,

As for the story of Chrysippus, we do not even know whether it played a part in Aeschylus' trilogy.[17] Lloyd-Jones thinks this probable, since there must be a reason why Apollo told Laius not to have children. Perhaps he is right, but it is not really important whether Aeschylus - or the author of the *Oedipodeia* - used the story. The only thing that matters is whether it was a fixed part of the Oedipus myth, a part that no poet could alter or ignore, like Oedipus' murder of his father and his marriage to his mother. This was certainly not the case. Concerning Chrysippus Bethe (2498) observes: 'Seine Sage ist an verschiedenen Orten und nach zwei verschiedenen Richtungen ausgebildet'. On the one hand, there is the story - even referred to by Thucydides - that he was killed by his

---

think of revivals, although the plays of Sophocles can only have been restaged at a lesser festival. In any case, it is hardly probable that the majority of Euripides' audience were thoroughly acquainted with all three tragedies.

Saïd's article is interesting, but her claim seems exaggerated. Why would Euripides have written a play that - as he himself could foresee - was more or less incomprehensible to part of his audience? Moreover, the audience's expectations were guided not merely by the tragedies *we* happen to know. Euripides, too, produced an *Antigone*, a play that probably preceded the *Phoenician Women*.

17. The controversy on the subject is of long standing. See Lamer's article in the *RE*. Recently the problem has been discussed by Rachel Aélion (181-185). She weighs the evidence accurately, but reaches no conclusion: 'Rien ne permet d'affirmer ou de nier qu'il (sc. Euripides) ait trouvé le motif de Chrysippos chez Eschyle'. See also Podlecki, 13-14. Hutchinson rejects the idea that the Chrysippus story was the subject of the first play: 'If Apollo gave the oracle because Laius had seduced Chrysippus, that incident ... must have occurred before the start of the play' (xxiii).

half-brothers Atreus and Thyestes, or by Atreus alone.[18] On the other hand, there was the tale of the abduction, but even here Laius could be dispensed with: in another version Zeus was the culprit.[19] And if Laius could be absent from a tale about Chrysippus, then Chrysippus could be absent from a tale about Laius. This was the poet's choice.

Lloyd-Jones maintains that an explicit reference to Laius' sin would have been impossible 'before the point at which it is established that Oedipus killed Laius'. And after that point it would be 'almost as undesirable' (123). However, we would do better to reverse this reasoning. If Sophocles had wanted to convey that Oedipus paid for his father's sin, he would have made a play in which it was *not* impossible or undesirable to make this clear. And when Lloyd-Jones assumes that Laius' guilt is hinted at two or three times, he is overlooking an essential point. Referring to vv. 1184-5 he observes: 'Why should Laius and Iocaste not have begotten Oedipus? The

---

18.   Thucydides 1.9. Other references in Pausanias 6.20.7; Sch. Euripides *Orestes* 4; Sch. *Iliad* B 105; Hyginus 85 and 243.

19.   Praxilla (Page *PMG* 751); cf. Clemens Alexandrinus *Protreptikos* 2.28. In Hyginus 271 Chrysippus is abducted by Theseus, supposedly a misrepresentation of ὁ Ζεύς in the Greek example.

In addition to Euripides' play *Chrysippus*, his abduction by Laius is also related in the hypothesis of the *Phoenician Women*, by Athenaeus (13.602 f.), Apollodorus (*Bibl.* 3.5.5), by Hyginus (85) and the scholiast ad *Phoen.* 1760, who claims Peisander as his source. According to this Peisander - whose identity is not clear - Chrysippus committed suicide out of shame. This version is of course incompatible with his death at the hands of his half-brothers. Hyginus (85), or his source, invented a means to combine the stories: Pelops made war at Laius and thus recuperated Chrysippus, who was afterwards killed by Atreus and Thyestes.

words have far more point if we recognize that Laius was warned beforehand' (122). And again with reference to Oedipus' words in vv. 1382-3: 'For him, the strongest possible proof of his impurity is his belonging to the race of Laius' (122). But how can this be a proof *for him*? Oedipus only knows what Iocasta has told him; he can have no added information from the *Seven*. How are we to explain the fact that he knows about Laius' sins? Or must we assume that Oedipus speaks the truth unwittingly? However, this would lead to the unacceptable view that, even at the end of the tragedy, the spectators are better informed about Oedipus' condition than Oedipus himself and that they are able to understand why he has suffered this fate, while he himself lacks the information to do so.[20]

If the audience added the affair with Chrysippus despite Sophocles' complete silence on the subject, and if Sophocles could only dissociate himself from Aeschylus by stating explicitly that Oedipus did *not* atone for any sin of his father, then the work of his predecessor must have been a heavy burden to bear. I believe that things may well have worked the other way round. If the older members of Sophocles' audience remembered Aeschylus' trilogy, they must have realized, more keenly than the others, that Sophocles did *not* deal with crime

---

20. In the second edition of his book Lloyd-Jones left his original text unaltered, but added an Epilogue and a number of notes. In a short note on p. 247 he agrees with Winnington-Ingram that Sophocles 'wished to concentrate upon the individual destiny of the hero, ...' (Winnington-Ingram 205). However, this small concession in no way concerns the methodical problems raised by his argument.

and punishment. And if Aeschylus' audience remembered the *Cypria*, they must have realized that he left out the stag and wondered why; this may have put them on the right track. I am quite aware that any remarks on an audience's response must be speculative, since there is no possible means of verification. But I do think that there was no sense in using the same mythic material over and over, unless the audience perceived what was new and different in the tragedy they were watching now.

Before rounding off this chapter with a few concluding remarks, I must deal with one more problem, namely the προαγών. Unfortunately, little is known about this happening, and the few available sources are not entirely clear. Thanks to Aeschines (*in Ctes.* 67) we are able to fix the date: the 8th of the month Elaphebolion, a few days before the Dionysia. Additional information is supplied by Aeschines' scholiast, while the *proagon* is referred to in the *Vita Euripidis* (ll. 45-48, ed. Budé), in Plato's *Symposium* 194 a-b and - it would appear - in the scholium on Aristophanes' *Wasps* 1109.[21] We do not know when the ceremony first took place. It was held in the Odeion (of Pericles), a building that was not completed until about 444 BC, but it may have been held elsewhere

---

21. It has been suggested by Hug, among others, that Plato is not describing the *proagon*, but Agathon's appearance at the festival proper. This, however, seems out of the question. As to the scholium on *Wasps* I have some doubts; cf. my appendix.

It is a matter of dispute whether Aristophanes, *Acharn.* 11, is referring to the *proagon* (see Rennie's comment ad loc.), but even if it is, this provides no new information.

before that year. As we know from the sources, the poet presented himself to the audience together with his actors and his chorus; no masks or costumes were worn. It is obvious that the theatre-goers-to-be were somehow informed about the plays to be put on, but we do not know the exact nature of this information. As Blume observes: 'Vor allem hätten wir gern gewußt, ob die Dichter ein Resümee ihrer Dramen gaben oder sich damit begnügten, die Titel der Stücke bekanntzugeben' (18). We would indeed like to know. If the poet actually gave a synopsis of his plots, the spectators would always have known what was going to happen - or rather, part of the spectators would have known, since the audience at the festival proper must have been far larger than at the *proagon*.

Since the sources offer no solution (see the appendix), we must rely on our common sense. I believe there are serious objections to the hypothesis that the tragedians exposed the plots of their plays. In the light of the paramount importance of the performance at the Dionysia, one may wonder why a poet would put all his cards on the table beforehand. Even when a plot was built on a well-known myth, there was plenty of room for suspense and surprise. At the performance of Sophocles' *Oedipus Tyrannus* the audience knew that Oedipus had killed his father and married his mother and that he would discover this during the play, but they had not the faintest idea *how* he would find out. The appearance of Tiresias for example must have created considerable suspense. The entire audience must have realized that the seer knew the truth, but also that it was too early for a real dénouement. How would Sophocles handle this? And later on, the appearance of the messenger from Corinth is as surprising to a spectator who

knows the story but does not know the plot, as it is to the
characters in the play. It is hard to imagine Sophocles giving
away such information to even part of his audience-to-be.

However, we can get somewhat further than this if we turn
to Euripides' divine prologue-speakers. These gods announce
what is going to happen but, as has often been observed, their
information is not always very precise. In *Ion* the plot does
not develop according to Apollo's intentions, as expressed by
Hermes in the prologue. The son is nearly killed by the
mother and then the mother by the son, before they recognize
each other. This recognition takes place in Delphi, and not, as
Apollo intended, later on in Athens. In *Bacchae* 50-52
Dionysus announces what he plans to do if the Thebans use
violence against the maenads in the mountains: he will fight
them at the head of his women. However, this is not the way
the god eventually takes his revenge. In *Hippolytus* Aphrodite
suggests that she herself will inform Theseus about Phaedra's
love and that Hippolytus will die before Phaedra. The result
is, as Barrett observes, that 'what she tells us does nothing to
give away the plot or destroy our interest: it serves if anything
to mislead and mystify, so that the way in which the plot
develops will come as a surprise' (164, ad 41-50). In *Trojan
Women* Poseidon does not mystify the audience, but the
information he gives is carefully portioned out. He only
mentions what has already happened, though this is not yet
known to Hecabe: Polyxena's death and Cassandra's allotment
to Agamemnon. But he does not announce the death of Astya-
nax, and the audience is unprepared for this shock when it
comes.

In all these cases information is withheld from the audience or false expectations are raised. This appears to be a deliberate stratagem designed to create suspense and to allow for subsequent surprise. Such a stratagem would be quite senseless if the poet gave away at the *proagon* what he suppressed in his prologues. Thus I consider it almost certain that the tragedians did *not* expose the plot of their plays.

Following this digression, I will conclude with a few remarks about the foreknowledge of the Athenian audience in the fifth century. First, they were familiar with the well-known myths. Second, the poet could rely on them to recall this knowledge when he appealed to it. And third, he could also be fairly sure that they would not take into account any information from outside the play if he did *not* invite them to do so.

Thus we must ask the following questions with respect to every tragedy. Was the plot based on a myth which was already well-known at the time of the first performance? If so, which facts were fundamental to that myth, and which were the variable details? In the following chapters I shall try to explain the importance of these questions, dealing first with Aeschylus' *Agamemnon*.

3. AESCHYLUS' *AGAMEMNON*

Three mythical tales play an important role in this tragedy: the sacrifice of Iphigenia, the meal of Thyestes and the murder of Agamemnon.[1] Two of these stories, the sacrifice and the meal, are concerned with the history prior to the play. They are already part of the past when the tragedy begins, while the murder still belongs to the future. All three of them are, of course, connected with Agamemnon's house, but they are not necessarily connected with each other. I shall therefore discuss each in turn.

First, the sacrifice of Iphigenia. Was this a well-known story in 458, the year of the play's first performance? We may assume that it was, as it had already been dealt with in the *Cypria* (p. 104 Allen), in ps.-Hesiod's *Catalogue of Women* (fr. 23a MW) and Stesichorus' *Oresteia* (215 *PMG*), by Pin-

---

1. It seems superfluous to argue that Aeschylus, like all other tragedians, assumed prior knowledge of the Trojan war, its cause, its course and its final outcome.

dar[2] and by Aeschylus himself in a tragedy *Iphigenia*. We need not assume that every Athenian in Aeschylus' audience was familiar with all these works. But the greater the number of testimonies, the more likely it is that the story was well-known apart from a particular source. There is, however, another argument in favour of this hypothesis.

Pindar refers to the slaughter of Iphigenia as a possible reason for Clytaemnestra's murderous deed, but he does so in such an oblique manner that no one would understand what happened, unless he knew the story beforehand. Pindar does not even make it clear that Iphigenia was Clytaemnestra's daughter nor that Agamemnon was responsible for her death; Artemis is not mentioned, nor is the voyage to Troy. Apparently Pindar expected his public to know the main facts of the story, as did Aeschylus, I believe, when he composed the parodos of his *Agamemnon*. He, too, appeals to his audience's prior knowledge, though less obviously than Pindar.

When the chorus quote Calchas' divination, his anxious words about a gruesome sacrifice that Artemis may demand (vv. 146-52) are no longer puzzling to them. They now know the outcome; they know that Artemis did demand a sacrifice and that the victim was Iphigenia. However, at the moment of delivery, this part of the prophecy *was* a riddle to the Greeks. It is only after Calchas has spoken a second time (vv. 198-201) that the Atreids realize which 'other sacrifice, one without precedent and law, without feast' (vv. 152-3) the seer

---

2. *Py.* 11, 22-23. The ode was probably composed in honour of a victory in 474 BC.

feared.[3] As for the spectator, if he knows the story he will understand the prophecy once the name of Artemis has been mentioned (v. 135). If he does not, he will have to wait till he can infer from Agamemnon's words in vv. 206-10 that the goddess demands the death of his daughter (εἰ τέχνον δαΐξω ... παρθενοσφάγοισιν). Meanwhile, however, the chorus has sung the so-called Hymn to Zeus, apparently inspired by their concern about the sacrifice and its consequences for Agamemnon.[4] The Hymn only makes sense to spectators who already know what the chorus know: that Agamemnon killed his daughter. To an audience without prior knowledge it would come too early.

There are three unvarying facts in the story of Iphigenia's sacrifice: Artemis demanded it, the voyage to Troy depended on it, and Agamemnon consented to it. We have already seen that the reason given for Artemis' demand might vary, and the

---

3. Apart from one exception (see p. 52) I quote Fraenkel's translation.

4. I am of course aware that the interpretation of vv. 176-83 in particular is controversial in this respect, as in most others. However, even those scholars who do not agree that the chorus are fearing for Agamemnon integrate the sacrifice into their interpretation. Smith, for example, denies that the chorus, while singing vv. 176-83, have Agamemnon in mind, but he does assume that the Hymn is inspired by the emotional tension caused even now by the horror of the sacrifice (13-14). Gagarin maintains that the Hymn has nothing to do with the sacrifice. The chorus are anxious over the fate of the expedition to Troy, but they hope that Zeus' law will see to it that the Trojans are punished. But there is, so he says, 'an ironic secondary application' (144), since the *audience* would probably also think of Agamemnon. And this is only possible if, as early as the Hymn, the audience understood that Agamemnon had committed a crime: the sacrifice of his daughter.

same is true of other details.[5] Even the rescue of Iphigenia, which was part of the story in earlier sources, could be left out. Pindar does not allude to it. In the *Agamemnon* none of the characters doubt that Iphigenia is dead, and Aeschylus does not allude to her survival as a priestess or a goddess.[6] This is natural enough since the sacrifice as a motive for the murder would be ambiguous if Iphigenia had not been really killed.

Secondly the meal of Thyestes. In the previous chapter I maintained that this story must have been known to the audience, since otherwise much of the Cassandra scene would

---

5. See ch. 2, pp. 31-2. In addition to the story of the stag and Aeschylus' version in the *Agamemnon*, there is also the reason mentioned in Euripides' *Iphigenia in Tauris* (20-24): Agamemnon once promised, in the year of Iphigenia's birth, to sacrifice the most beautiful thing the year would give him, and now the goddess is holding him to his promise. Apollodorus (*Epit.* 3.21) suggests still another reason: Artemis was angry because Atreus did not sacrifice the golden lamb to her. But if a poet had no need for a reason, he could leave it out altogether, as Euripides did in his *Iphigenia in Aulis*.

6. I do not consider v. 247 (τὰ δ' ἔνθεν οὔτ' εἶδον οὔτ' ἐννέπω) such a hint; cf. Fraenkel 141 n. 3. Lattimore (40) argues: '...as I suppose, both Aeschylus and his audience well understood that the god did intervene, and Iphigeneia was not sacrificed at all but miraculously, and secretly, rescued and transformed'. The wording of this sentence is strange: did Aeschylus 'understand' that his own version of the myth was incomplete? As for the audience, they may have remembered the story of Iphigenia's rescue, but they probably accepted that, for the purpose of this play, she was dead. In any case, I believe it wrong to integrate the rescue into our interpretation, as Lattimore does: 'As in some versions of the story of Troy, according to which Helen never fled with Paris at all, so in this case, the slaughtered Iphigeneia would be a wraith, an illusion, whose fictitious quality did nothing to diminish the deadly effect' (41).

have been a riddle to them. The tale in itself does not leave much room for variable details and its previous history is scarcely referred to. As is clear from vv. 1192-3, Aeschylus expected his spectators to know that Thyestes' adultery was the primary sin.[7] This knowledge enabled them to understand that Aegisthus (vv. 1585-6) is disguising the truth. But Thyestes' guilt does not really matter in this play. Whatever he did, it pales into insignificance before the gruesome murder of his innocent children.

As to the aftermath of Atreus' crime, the birth and the career of Aegisthus clearly belonged to the varying details. Of course he is always the son of Thyestes, but Aeschylus has discarded the fanciful story of Thyestes' incest with his daughter and Aegisthus' subsequent revenge on Atreus himself.[8] In this play Aegisthus wants to punish Agamemnon for what Atreus has done. This desire for revenge is hardly compatible with any previous revenge on the sinner himself.

We come now to the murder of Agamemnon. This was undoubtedly a well-known story. It is recounted in the *Odyssey*, not once but several times: by Nestor to Telemachus (γ 193-94; 262-75), by Menelaus (who quotes the words of Proteus) to Telemachus (δ 512-37) and by Agamemnon him-

---

7. Cf. ch. 2 n. 4.

8. The story is told by Apollodorus (*Epit.* 2.14) and Hyginus (88), and it must have been the subject of several tragedies; cf. Radt, 239-40. However, in Aeschylus' play Aegisthus had already been born when his brothers were slaughtered by Atreus (vv. 1605-6). It is not inconceivable that the story of the incest was invented by one of the tragedians. In that case Aeschylus did not discard it, but may simply have been unaware of it.

self, in the nether world, to Odysseus (λ 405-34). Moreover, it had been dealt with by ps.-Hesiod (*Catalogue* fr. 23a), in the *Nostoi*, in Stesichorus' *Oresteia* and in the above-mentioned Pindaric ode. Very few features of the tale are actually fixed. There is always the adulterous love of Aegisthus and Clytaemnestra, but the place and circumstances of the murder may differ, and the actual killing may be done either by Aegisthus or by Clytaemnestra. The death of Cassandra, while perhaps not fixed, seems to have been a regular component.

One detail which clearly did vary is the motive for the murder. The presence of Aegisthus in the palace and his affair with Agamemnon's wife would in itself seem reason enough, and it is in fact the only reason suggested in the *Odyssey*. We have no information on the subject from Hesiod, the *Nostoi* or Stesichorus' poem. Pindar does not resolve the question: was it Iphigenia? was it the bed Clytaemnestra shared with Aegisthus? Another possible motive is the fact that Agamemnon brings home his mistress, a motive which, for understandable reasons, gets all the weight in Euripides' *Trojan Women* (cf. pp. 28-9). And then there is the revenge on Atreus' son, which may form a personal incentive for Aegisthus.

As we have seen above, the three tales need not be connected. Since the motive for the murder is a floating detail, there is not necessarily any connection between the murder and the sacrifice, nor between the murder and Atreus' sin. Thus the audience of Aeschylus' *Agamemnon*, on hearing the prologue, knew what would happen during the play: Agamemnon would come home and would meet his death. But they had no reason to suppose that the recent and the more distant past would play such a prominent role. It may be objected that perhaps they expected the tragedian to introduce the meal of Thyestes, as it was typically Aeschylean to deal with the sins of several generations. But is this actually so?

In her book *Time in Greek Tragedy* Mme de Romilly argues: 'We know that in almost all the plays of Aeschylus punishment is made to bear on the children and grandchildren of the person who committed the evil deed' (63). I contend that this is simply not true. Which plays does she mean? The *Oresteia* of course and the *Labdacid* trilogy, but it does not apply to the *Prometheia*, the *Persians* or the *Danaid* trilogy. Nor does the lost work provide any indication that Aeschylus specialized in 'family-guilt'; indeed how could he, since families like the Atreids and the Labdacids are actually rare. When Aeschylus wrote a play about Achilles, Ajax or Philoctetes, no guilty fathers were at his disposal. Thus the family curse can hardly have been his trademark.

In my discussion of certain passages of Aeschylus' *Agamemnon*, the starting point will be a statement from Anne Lebeck's much-praised study of the *Oresteia*: 'The philologist ... should give free rein to all possibilities and associations, ultimately selecting as many as form part of a larger pattern and contribute to the meaning of the total work' (*Introduction* 3). However, we must bear in mind that the philologist was not Aeschylus' intended public. If the philologist's associations cannot have occurred to the original audience, I think they ought to be checked. Even if they appear to contribute 'to the meaning of the total work', they may in reality thwart the poet's intention. I realize that it is difficult to know what was in the mind of the audience, but we must at least try to weigh the evidence.

Let us now turn to the text. When the *parodos* starts, the audience know that the war has ended and they may expect that the chorus have come to celebrate the victory and the victor. Instead, the beginning of the war is the subject of their song. The Atreids launched the expedition against Troy

μέγαν ἐκ θυμοῦ κλάζοντες Ἄρη,
τρόπον αἰγυπιῶν
οἵτ' ἐκπατίοις ἄλγεσι παίδων
ὕπατοι λεχέων στροφοδινοῦνται
πτερύγων ἐρετμοῖσιν ἐρεσσόμενοι,
δεμνιοτήρη
πόνον ὀρταλίχων ὀλέσαντες·
ὕπατος δ' ἀΐων ἤ τις Ἀπόλλων
ἤ Πὰν ἤ Ζεὺς
οἰωνόθροον γόον ὀξυβόαν,
τῶν δὲ μετοίκων * * * * * *,
ὑστερόποινον
πέμπει παραβᾶσιν Ἐρινύν.
οὕτω δ' Ἀτρέως παῖδας ὁ κρείσσων
ἐπ' Ἀλεξάνδρωι πέμπει ξένιος
Ζεύς ...

'shouting from an angry heart the cry for a mighty war, like vultures that, in extreme (?) grief for their children, high above their bed circle round and round, rowing with the oars of their wings, having lost the couch-keeping labour they had spent over their nestlings; but one in the height, Apollo, it may be, or Pan or Zeus, hearing the shrill cry of the birds' lament, and <feeling great compassion for> the denizens in his realm, sends on the transgressors her who brings punishment though late, Erinys. Even so the sons of

Atreus are sent by the mightier one against Alexandros, by Zeus, guardian of guest-law...' (vv. 48-62).

To Lebeck this simile 'reflects the paradox of right and wrong that runs throughout the trilogy. Paris is guilty of stealing Helen; Agamemnon is no less guilty. Like the nameless wrongdoers punished in the simile (59), he has taken a child from its parent' (9). Here I have my doubts about the philologist's associations. Full knowledge of the parodos impresses upon the reader the terrible importance of the sacrifice, but on hearing vv. 48-62, the first-time spectator has no reason to think of Iphigenia, since there is no indication as yet that the sacrifice will play any role at all. It is true that the Atreids are bereft of a woman, while the birds are bereft of their children. But do two birds, robbed of their nestlings by 'nameless wrongdoers', suggest a mother whose daughter has been killed by her husband? I think not. The association may 'form part of a larger pattern', but for the spectator this pattern is set out only gradually.

Some fifty lines later we are again confronted with two birds, eagles this time, identified by Calchas as the Atreids. These birds are not victims, but birds of omen and merciless killers of a pregnant hare. Calchas foretells the destruction of Troy, but fears that Artemis is angry with the eagles and will detain the Greek ships

σπευδομένα θυσίαν ἑτέ-
ραν ἄνομόν τιν' ἄδαιτον,
νεικέων τέκτονα σύμφυτον οὐ δεισ-
ήνορα· μίμνει γὰρ φοβερὰ παλίνορτος
οἰκονόμος δολία, μνάμων Μῆνις τεκνόποινος.

'in her eagerness to bring about another sacrifice, one without precedent and law, without a feast, a worker of quarrels, born together with it, without fear of the husband; for there abides a terrible, ever re-arising, treacherous housekeeper; unforgetting, child-avenging Wrath' (151-5).

My rendering is Fraenkel's except for the word σύμφυτον, as I am convinced that his translation of this adjective is impossible. He renders it twice: 'born in the house and grown one with it', but neither translation will do. σύμφυτος does not mean 'born in' but 'born together with'. The age of the elders (v. 106) has been born together with themselves. If someone possesses σύμφυτος ἀρετή, 'innate virtue', that virtue has been born *with* him, and not at some moment during his life; it exists as long as he himself has existed. However, it is clear that Aeschylus' 'worker of quarrels' has not existed as long as the house.

Fraenkel's second rendering, 'grown one with it', while theoretically possible, is improbable in poetry and does not fit the context. Growing together is a gradual process. In this case the sacrifice would mark the starting-point of such a process, not its completion. We would expect Calchas to say 'a worker of quarrels that *will* grow one with the house' and not 'that *has* grown one with it'. And finally it is quite arbitrary to connect συμ- with a word that is not found in the Greek.[9]

---

9. For an extensive discussion of the meaning of σύμφυτος, see my article mentioned in the bibliography.

I now turn to Lebeck's comment on these lines: 'The words θυσίαν ἑτέραν do refer back to the omen. However, they also evoke the first such sacrifice of young within the house of Atreus, the festal banquet served Thyestes. This is suggested by the lines that follow. The new sacrifice is said to be innate (σύμφυτον, 153), an architect of strife for Atreus' house (νεικέων τέκτονα, 153), because of the curse passed from generation to generation. The child-avenging fury (μῆνις τεκνόποινος, 155) which waits within is more than vengeance for the murder of Iphigenia. It is an older μῆνις as well, one with long memory (μνάμων), recurrent (παλίνορτος)' (34).

Lebeck is right, of course, when she says that the words ἑτέραν θυσίαν refer back to the omen. Aeschylus does not leave any doubt about that, since the gruesome meal of the eagles - and this is noteworthy - is also described as a sacrifice (θυομένοισιν, 137). But did these words really evoke in Aeschylus' audience the thought of the 'festal banquet served Thyestes'? Did they appeal to the spectators' prior knowledge? Each detail is fully comprehensible without such associations, and I find Lebeck's arguments in favour of them dubious and somewhat misleading, as she does not make always clear what is in the Greek and what is her own interpretation.

As I maintained above, σύμφυτος cannot mean 'innate', unless the thing born is born together with its bearer. The sacrifice is not said to be an architect of strife *for Atreus' house*: no such reference to the previous generation is to be found in the text, let alone Lebeck's addition 'because of the curse passed from generation to generation'. Moreover, the adjective δεισήνορα, which suggests Clytaemnestra's murder of her husband, interferes with the association with Thyestes' meal. In short, I believe that the words νεικέων τέκτονα σύμφυτον οὐ δεισήνορα do not even make sense in connection with the sin of Atreus.

In the next sentence, the adjective μνάμων is completely justified by the length of the Trojan war, as is παλίνορτος; this suggests that the μῆνις will be extreme at the time the sacrifice is made, but since she is powerless for the moment, she will have to wait, arising again when the opportunity for revenge presents itself. I agree that, taken in isolation, both adjectives might refer to what happened in the past, but the context - in particular the particle γάρ - does not favour such a reference. The sentence is meant to explain the previous one and, as I maintained above, this previous sentence cannot have anything to do with Thyestes' children.

However, these two examples are concerned only with secondary associations. A more important point is Lebeck's answer to the question: Why does Artemis demand the sacrifice? This time she offers only one explanation: 'In order that Agamemnon atone for the guilt of his father she demands "another sacrifice" and renders him guilty of his father's crime' (35). In my opinion this interpretation obscures the meaning of the omen. According to Calchas, the eagles represent the Atreids, and since the omen's favourable part spells the destruction of Priam's town, the hare must represent Troy. But there is also an unfavourable part and now, if Lebeck were right, all of a sudden the eagles would symbolize Atreus' act of aggression and the hare the young sons of Thyestes. This would leave the omen unclear. Moreover, Agamemnon's moral dilemma would lose much of its weight, since - as in the case of the stag - there would be a prior guilt to be atoned for. But this is not all. Lebeck's interpretation is a reader's interpretation, which can hardly have occurred to spectators. She herself pays little attention to the question. She is aware, of course, that the curse is not presented until late in the play, but she dismisses the problem as irrelevant: 'There is no direct allusion to the crimes of Atreus and Thyestes prior to the Cassandra scene. However, preparation for the story and for its prominence at the end of the play begins in the parodos and continues in the first and second stasimon' (176 n. 19). And, on the next page: '...the curse does make its presence felt from the beginning of the play. The entire drama is a gradual revelation of things dimly perceived at first...' (n. 25). However, what exactly does this mean?

'Preparation' is a convenient catch word, but how does it work and does it bear on this special case? In exploring the matter it seems useful to follow Pütz, who distinguishes between 'announcement' (*Ankündigung*) and 'indication' (*Andeutung*).[10] Announcement is explicit: a seer may foretell the future or another character may announce what he is planning and unfold his expectations. In the case of a prophecy the audience know for sure what is going to happen since, in tragedies at least, prophecies always come true. When the third witch has said 'All hail Macbeth, that shalt be king

---

10. Perhaps 'allusion' would be a better translation of the German 'Andeutung'. But since Lebeck uses this word in her note and Furley (infra 60-1) uses the adjective 'allusive', I thought it better to avoid confusion.

hereafter', the spectators are prepared for the future kingship of Macbeth, though they do not know as yet *how* he will acquire it. On the other hand, human plans and expectations may be frustrated. When Macbeth orders the murder of Banquo and his son, the audience are prepared for the attempted assassination, but they do not know whether it will succeed. However, in both cases this kind of preparation makes the audience expect a definite event: Macbeth will be king and Banquo will be attacked by murderers.

'Indication' is implicit: nothing definite is announced but the audience get the feeling that there is something brewing, that some kind of disaster is imminent. Indications are, as Pütz has it: '...vieldeutig und müssen oft mehr empfunden als verstanden werden. Sie weisen vage in eine Richtung und erwecken Vermutungen und Affekte. Eine Bühnenfigur z.B. sinniert über die Zeit und bangt um die Zukunft. *Was* diese bringt oder bringen könnte, wird nicht formuliert: nur *daß* sie unheilschwanger ist, kommt zum Ausdruck' (95).

As an example of indication, Pütz quotes the following words of Gretchen in Goethe's *Faust*:

> Es wird mir so, ich weiß nicht wie -
> Ich wollt', die Mutter käm' nach Haus,
> Mir läuft ein Schauer übern ganzen Leib.[11]

He comments: 'Stimmungen, die zwar auf Kommendes deuten, können dennoch so undeutlich sein, daß sie sich nicht einmal benennen lassen'. Gretchen does not understand that both love and sheer evil make her shudder.

---

11. *Faust*, vv. 2755-7. Pütz 103, in the section called *Stimmungen*.

In this comment Pütz makes no clear distinction between characters and audience; he seems to be thinking mainly of Gretchen. However, the audience have more information at their disposal. They know about Faust and Mephisto, they know that Faust lusts for Gretchen and that he, together with Mephisto, has been in her room. This is reason enough to expect disaster, and Gretchen's confusion does perhaps little to strengthen this expectation. It rather indicates that she has already been captured in the net of love and evil. Her own love is stirring in her (vv. 2678-83), and she feels the love of Faust and the evil of Mephisto lingering in her room.

In the same section Pütz mentions the third stasimon of the *Agamemnon*. Before the murder of the king 'drückt der Chor seine "Angst" (δεῖμα) aus und überträgt sie auf das Publikum. Ganz im Sinne der Andeutung gibt die Stimmung keine eindeutige Information' (100). This time Pütz does account for the impact on the audience, but not quite satisfactorily. It is true that the chorus are beset by a nameless fear, but the spectators *know* that Agamemnon will be killed. The anguish of the chorus may add to the horror and the suspense felt by the audience, but it does not really alter their expectations. Right from the beginning their prior knowledge has prepared them for Agamemnon's death.[12]

We now turn again to the preparation referred to by Lebeck. First of all we must remember that, in general, spectators are prepared for things that are going to *happen*: Macbeth

---

12. Pütz supposes that an audience may forget what they know; see my quotation on p. 100. This may be the reason that he does not pay much attention to prior knowledge.

will be king, Banquo will be attacked, Gretchen will meet
with evil. However, Lebeck is referring to preparation for
information which will subsequently be supplied: the revelation of a past event which may contribute to our understanding of what happened afterwards and what is happening now.
How is an audience prepared for information to come?

A character may say that he is expecting someone who will
bring him news. When, for example, Oedipus (*Oedipus Tyrannus* 69-75) wonders why Creon has not yet returned from
Delphi, the audience are prepared, by announcement, for
Creon's arrival and for the supply of fresh information. Need-
less to say, such instances are irrelevant here. Pütz (137)
refers to the watchman in the *Agamemnon*, who does not want
to speak of the situation in the house of his masters: 'As for
the rest, I am silent' (v. 36). In this case, no supply of information is announced, but a secret is alluded to, which may be
revealed in the course of the play. However, here again we
must reckon with the audience's prior knowledge. As we have
seen, the murder of Agamemnon was inextricably linked to
Clytaemnestra's adultery. It will have been clear to the spectators that the watchman is hinting at this adultery, as he did
earlier in vv. 18-19. His words do not prepare the audience for
the revelation of a secret, but rather suggest that the adultery,
though people are afraid to mention it, is nevertheless an open
secret. The same holds true for the chorus' words to the
herald: 'Silence has long been my remedy against harm' (v.
548). The chorus, too, know what is going on and it is important that the audience realize this. Clytaemnestra's welcoming
speech is all the more terrifying when we are aware that

everyone on stage - with the exception of Agamemnon - must know she is lying.[13]

Though the example of the watchman is not entirely satisfactory, it is certainly true to say that an audience may be prepared for information by a character's refusal to speak out. But even without such a refusal, they may feel that certain information is lacking, simply because they cannot fully understand what is happening or what is being said. We find an interesting example of this in Albee's *Who is afraid of Virginia Woolf?* From the very beginning, there is something strange and puzzling about the way Martha and George talk about their absent son. The playgoers probably feel that there is some unknown factor here, perhaps an appalling secret of some kind involving this son, and expect it to be revealed before the end of the play. Some of them may suspect the truth before it is actually revealed, while others may not; but all of them are, during a certain time, being prepared for further information on the subject.

We now return to Thyestes. If Artemis' anger were really connected with Thyestes' meal, there are two possibilities: either the audience did already understand, or they did not. If they did, it could only be because the anger of the goddess, incomprehensible as it was, appealed to their prior knowledge and forced them to search for a reason outside the context of

---

13. Lloyd-Jones assumes that Agamemnon does know: 'it seems clear that rumours of what is going on at home have found their way to him' (1962, 195). It does not, however, seem clear to me. In real life such rumours often do reach the person in question, but there is no indication whatsoever in the text that it happened in this tragedy.

the Trojan war. This seems to me rather far-fetched; in any case, this cannot be what Lebeck means, since she does not take foreknowledge into account. Moreover this would be incompatible with her remark on preparation: once the spectators consciously incorporated the story of Thyestes into their interpretation, the preparatory phase was in effect over.

This leaves us with the second possibility: the audience did *not* understand why Artemis was angry, and they had to wait some 1000 lines until the riddle was solved by Cassandra. But did she actually solve it? Lebeck does not answer the question, but since she does not mention the parodos in her discussion of the Cassandra scene, she apparently does not detect any connection between the utterances of the prophetess and the sacrifice. This is only natural, for Cassandra does not refer even once to Iphigenia and Aulis or to Artemis and the omen. I think it, therefore, nearly impossible that her revelations enabled the audience to understand - in retrospect - why Artemis demanded the sacrifice. Lebeck's remarks on 'preparation' and 'gradual revelation' may suggest that attention is paid to the spectator, but actually they offer no explanation whatsoever.

I realize that Lebeck is not the only scholar who tends to neglect the spectator. Others either fail to mention the problem, or handle it unsatisfactorily. Furley, for instance, argues that the μῆνις in v. 155 refers exclusively to the curse that originated in Thyestes' meal. Calchas is afraid that the murder of Thyestes' children, still unavenged, will now take its toll: the life of Iphigenia. Furley adds that 'the reference to the family curse is still allusive in these two lines of Calchas' divination. By the end of the play it has become quite explicit through the clairvoyance of the other seer in the play, Cassandra' (113). However, it does *not* become explicit that there was any connection between the family curse and Artemis' demand. Here again the relevant questions go unanswered. Did the audience understand the allusion because of their prior knowledge, or not? And if not, did they understand it later on? But how and when?

We come now to Lloyd-Jones, who does not connect Thyestes' meal with Artemis' anger, but does argue that Agamemnon decides to sacrifice Iphigenia because 'Zeus sends Ate to take away his judgement' (1962, 199). In this way the god forces him to commit a crime in order that he will be murdered and atone for his father's sin. Unlike Lebeck and Furley, Lloyd-Jones at times tries to take the spectators into account. These attempts are, however, not entirely satisfactory, as will be clear from the following examples.

According to Lloyd-Jones, when the chorus invoke the supreme god in the Hymn to Zeus, they do so because only Zeus can help Agamemnon. Then he adds: 'Yet the Chorus does not appear at all confident that such aid will be forthcoming. "Why not?", the audience may wonder. The Chorus gives no indication of the reason for its fears; at this point, the audience can only ponder on the riddling final words of the prophecy of Calchas. But, in the light of a full knowledge of the play, the reader may well wonder, "Will aid from Zeus be forthcoming for the son of Atreus?"' (191). With respect to this paragraph we must remember first of all that the *reader*, 'in the light of a full knowledge of the play', does not wonder at all, since he knows exactly what is going to happen. And why would the *audience* wonder? They know that Iphigenia has been sacrificed, they know that Agamemnon is going to be murdered, so the final words of Calchas can hardly be riddling to them. Nor can they be surprised at the chorus' anxiety. The chorus do not know what will happen, but they realize that the final part of the prophecy contains a menace that continues to cloud the future; the death of Iphigenia is still unavenged.

Later on, when discussing the Cassandra scene, Lloyd-Jones returns to the subject: 'Since the narrative of the prophecy of Calchas, the audience has felt that there is some dark factor in the situation which has only been hinted at; something which if known would do more to explain the sinister forebodings of the Chorus than any vague talk of murmurs in the city against the princes' (198). And, on the same page: 'Cassandra supplies us, first obscurely and later at the climax explicitly, with the vital piece of information that gives the missing clue for which we have so long been seeking'. Apparently the 'we' in the second quotation is a shorthand notation for 'the spectators', and Lloyd-Jones seems to consider it an established fact that they have felt all along that they lack a 'vital piece of information'. In fact, however, he is ascribing to the audience the lack of understanding which fits his interpretation of the play. I agree that 'vague talk of murmurs in the city' does not sufficiently explain the chorus' anguish, but why suggest that no other explanation has been offered? Agamemnon has killed his daughter and the child-avenging Wrath is waiting at home. Greek blood has been spilled for an adulterous woman and the chorus are convinced that the gods resent it:

τῶν πολυκτόνων γὰρ οὐκ ἄσκοποι
θεοί· κελαιναὶ δ' Ἐρινύες χρόνωι
τυχηρὸν ὄντ' ἄνευ δίκας
    παλιντυχεῖ τριβᾶι βίου
τιθεῖσ' ἀμαυρόν, ἐν δ' ἀί-
    στοις τελέθοντος οὔτις ἀλκά.

'For the gods are not unwatchful of those who cause much bloodshed; and the dark Erinyes in the course of time, when a man is
prosperous without justice, by wearing away his life in a reverse of
fortune render him faint and dim; and when he is among the van-
ished, there is no help.' (vv. 461-7)

They know that Clytaemnestra has a lover and that her wel-
come was entirely false. All this seems quite enough to
explain the chorus' fear, and I fail to see how the audience
could feel puzzled, as in the above-mentioned play by Albee.

And this is not all. In the case of *Who is afraid of Virginia
Woolf?* there is a clear solution to the riddle of the son.
Towards the end of the play the audience are told that he
never existed, except in the minds of Martha and George. But
do we find in the Cassandra scene any clue to Lloyd-Jones'
interpretation? If Aeschylus wanted to make it clear to us that
Zeus, in order to avenge Thyestes' children, took away Agamemnon's senses by sending him *Ate*, Cassandra would have
been an excellent mouthpiece: as a prophetess, she is the only
character who can know such things and present the audience
with an authoritative explanation. However, Cassandra says
nothing of the kind; she does not even make the faintest
suggestion. She refers to a good many subjects: the adultery of
Thyestes and the slaughter of his children, the liaison of
Clytaemnestra and Aegisthus, the imminent murder of Aga-

memnon and herself, Orestes' vengeance in the future, the destruction of Troy and the fate imposed on her by Apollo. But references to Aulis and the sacrifice are conspicuous by their absence. Moreover, she does not mention any god (either Zeus or Artemis) as an avenging power, but only the Erinyes who dwell in the house. If Aeschylus mystified his audience, the Cassandra scene does little to dissipate this mystification.[14] Lloyd-Jones' interpretation is the construction of a reader, one which cannot have occurred to the audience.

There is, I believe, no need for further examples. The authors discussed above are not of the same opinion, but they do have one thing in common: they all integrate the story of Thyestes into their interpretation long before it is introduced by Aeschylus in his play. According to all three, Agamemnon is forced or tempted into sinning in order to atone for his father's sin. But they all fail to account for the spectators: did *they* realize that Iphigenia was sacrificed because of Thyestes' children, and if so, when and how did this realization dawn? On hearing Cassandra, did they actually think to themselves: now at last I understand why Artemis was angry or why Agamemnon went mad? And even if they did, we must still ask ourselves why Aeschylus postponed his explanation for so long. Surely he must have had a reason for doing so? How-

---

14. Nor does the amoebaion (vv. 1407-1576) between the chorus and Clytaemnestra do so. The chorus eventually recognize that the sacrifice is a just grievance (δύσμαχα δ' ἐστὶ κρῖναι, v. 1561). However, it is not the sacrifice but the murder of the king that they, and Clytaemnestra, connect with the δαίμων or the ἀλάστωρ of the house.

ever, since all these questions have gone unanswered, I think that there is only one possible conclusion. Aeschylus did not refer to the sin of Agamemnon's father until the Cassandra scene because he wanted his audience to understand the previous part of the play *without having recourse to Thyestes' meal.*

Although I do not deny that there is some connection between Atreus' sin and the sacrifice, it is less clear-cut than the readers' interpretations will have it. If we did not know about Thyestes, we could still understand what happened at Aulis and why the chorus is continuously afraid. Cassandra does not explain what was inexplicable hitherto, but she does add a new dimension. Agamemnon, as Lebeck rightly remarks, has repeated his father's crime and the audience, on hearing Cassandra, may well feel that the evil powers in the house have something to do with his decision to shed blood, a decision that will generate new bloodshed. The sin of the father is not simply visited upon the son, though that is what Aegisthus thinks, nor is it visited upon him circuitously by forcing him into guilt. But coming from the family he does, he could hardly be expected to respect human life. Though this is never made explicit, it is suggested by the similarity of the crimes: the killing of young and innocent life that belongs to the family.

The Erinyes, Cassandra says (vv. 1186-90), never leave the house. But this 'never' does not cover the whole future. Eventually they will leave, when Orestes - unlike his father - is actually forced into sinning. The gods ordained his crime and the gods safeguard him from destruction.

4. DRAMATIC IRONY

The romanticists, as Sedgewick puts it, 'juggle with irony until the word loses meaning; they seem to vary the sense they put upon it, according as their humours and conceits may govern' (15).[1] This juggling act has continued to the present day, as a few selected examples will show. 'Drama is ... as Burke might say, the dancing of the ironic-dialectical attitude' (States 23). 'Irony ... is the force to which all of the clear moments of reversal we can confidently call peripeties, and all of the smaller things we call ironies of speech, bear a *vital* synecdochic relationship' (States 27). 'And the purged or purified state in which one is left at the end of a great tragedy is an ironic mood in which good and evil, triumph and disaster, are somehow balanced, harmonized and transcended' (Sharpe xiii). 'Why, a Greek tragedy is all Ironical; it is Ironical in its very nature' (J.A.K. Thomson, quoted by Sharpe, 28). And finally: 'But irony is a complex phenomenon

---

1. For a description of the history of the concept 'irony' see the books by Sedgewick, Behler and Muecke mentioned in the bibliography.

which is not easy to define, and is perhaps best left undefined'
(Kells 17).

Small wonder, then, that some authors object to the indis-
criminate use of the concept of irony. Muecke, for instance,
attacks 'those who refuse to define irony' and then continues:
'But of all those who make it difficult to be clear about irony
the worst are those who, being themselves both vague about
irony and afraid of being thought too simple-minded to detect
its presence, exploit the same qualities in their readers by
making such prudently unspecific remarks as 'the obvious
ironies of this passage...' But if one is not prepared to call the
bluff of these ironiphiles the word 'irony' will retreat further
into the conceptual fog that already half obscures it' (11). This
'conceptual fog' is dense indeed. Where the interpretation of
drama is concerned - and Greek tragedy in particular - it
originated in Thirlwall's famous article *On the Irony of
Sophocles*.

Thirlwall was undoubtedly influenced by the German
romanticists when he set the ironic trend. In his view there is
irony in 'the contrast between the appearance of good and the
reality of evil' (500), as well as in the opposite contrast. It is
understandable that he should call this irony, but when he
discusses the individual tragedies, he seems to be using the
term irony in a wide variety of ways. It goes without saying
that the *Oedipus Tyrannus* is an example of the first contrast.
But is *Ajax* an example of the second? Thirlwall's argument,
which appears at the end of his discussion of the play, runs as
follows: 'And thus the contrast between the appearance and
the reality is completed ... At the beginning we saw the hero
in the depth of degradation, an object of mockery and of pity:

this was the effect of his inordinate self-esteem, of his over-weening confidence in his own strength. But out of his humiliation, his anguish, and despair, issues a higher degree of happiness and renown than he had ever hoped to attain. He closes his career at peace with the gods: his incomparable merit is acknowledged by the rival whose success had wounded his pride: he leaves a name behind him which shall be remembered and revered to the latest generations' (524-5). It should be noted that here the irony is entirely dependent on the interpretation. I, for one, fail to detect either a 'higher degree of happiness' or Ajax' 'peace with the gods'; and as for his renown, he can only enjoy it in the nether world. But even if we accept Thirlwall's interpretation of the play's meaning, the contrast between appearance and reality is not comparable to that in the *Oedipus Tyrannus*. Oedipus' happiness has been built on quicksand all along; Ajax' distress is real enough. The happiness postulated by Thirlwall follows upon it; the two do not coexist. It is, therefore, singularly unenlightening to attach the same label to these contrasts, and to two such different plays.

However, Thirlwall has other ironies in store, such as the irony that manifests itself when two people, both of whom are in the right, appear before a judge: '...here the irony lies not in the demeanor of the judge, but is deeply seated in the case itself, which seems to favour each of the litigants, but really eludes them both' (490). Thirlwall finds this form of irony in *Antigone*, since in his view right and wrong are equally divided between Creon and Antigone. Here again the irony is based on his interpretation, an interpretation that has been rejected by many students of Sophocles. In any case, it seems rather arbitrary to call this irony. Thirlwall himself admits that it is 'totally different' from the previous examples. But what is gained by using the same word for totally different phenomena?

In Thirlwall's analysis of *Philoctetes* we read: '...the poet himself preserves an ironical composure, and while he excites our esteem and pity for the suffering hero, guards us against sharing the detestation Philoctetes feels for the authors of his calamity' (532). Thirlwall's treatment of his material is somewhat high-handed. He seems to be saying 'this is my interpretation and I choose to call this ironical'. Nevertheless, his influence has been enormous, and the concept of irony has gained a place in the interpretation of drama. Only Campbell has tried to turn the tide, objecting to 'straining the application of a term' (131). But his counterattack failed, and scholars have continued to discuss the role of irony in Greek drama, with special reference to Sophocles.[2] Winnington-Ingram, for instance, assures us: 'Sophocles is recognized as the supreme ironist, which is something not to be forgotten when we seek to understand his heroes and his gods' (329). And indeed we meet the concept all over his book: irony, tragic irony, dramatic irony, irony of circumstance, Sophoclean irony; ironies inherent in all kinds of situations.

---

2.   According to Rosenmeyer (32 n. 9) '...William Empson, in a review of Booth, has urged a return to the notion of irony as social subterfuge and nothing else: *New York Review of Books* 22, 10 (June 12, 1975) 37-39'. I am inclined to side with Empson, but I realize that it is perhaps now too late (cf. Szlezák, 9).

Much as I admire Winnington-Ingram's book, I do not feel that thinking of Sophocles as a 'supreme ironist' adds anything to my understanding of his tragedies. However, it is not my intention to crusade against the proliferation of the term in general. I will concentrate on the concept of 'dramatic irony' as it is defined in the following quotations:

- '(Dramatic ironies) arise immediately the audience is aware of something of which at least one character on stage is ignorant' (Dawson 40).

- '...we could say that dramatic irony is the exploitation by the playwright of situations, natural or artificial, in which one or more characters are unaware of the true state of things; the exploitation may, but need not, involve the use of language with double meaning' (Kirkwood 249).[3]

- 'Wir werden den Begriff "dramatische Ironie" auf jene ironischen Widersprüche einschränken, die sich aus der Interferenz des inneren und äußeren Kommunikationssystems ergeben. Sie tritt immer dann auf, wenn die sprachliche Äußerung oder das außersprachliche Verhalten einer Figur für den Rezipienten aufgrund seiner überlegenen Informiertheit eine der Intention der Figur widersprechende Zusatzbedeutung erhält' (Pfister 88).

---

3. For the distinction between 'natural' and 'artificial' see Kirkwood 251: 'We have distinguished between the "naturally ironical" situation - Oedipus unknowingly in pursuit of himself, Deianeira unwittingly destroying what she seeks to keep - and the contrived irony wherein a conscious deception is practiced: the deception of Philoctetes by Neoptolemus, of Clytemnestra by the henchman of Orestes, of Aegisthus by Electra and Orestes'.

- 'Dramatic irony, in brief, is the sense of contradiction felt by spectators of a drama who see a character acting in ignorance of his condition' (Sedgewick 49).

Pfister's observation that his description of the phenomenon agrees, in broad outlines, with Thirlwall's Sophoclean irony is not entirely justified. No doubt the use of the term dramatic irony was inspired by Thirlwall, but in Pfister's definition - as in the others - the range of the concept is considerably restricted.[4] Moreover, it has been objectified, since in principle it is no longer dependent on interpretation, as in Thirlwall's case. The common denominator in all these definitions is knowledge: there is something which the spectators are aware of, but which is unknown to at least one of the characters on stage. This knowledge determines their response to what they see and hear; verbal irony only enhances and sharpens an awareness that has been there all along.

As for verbal irony, Kirkwood's definition is less restricted than that of Pfister. According to the latter, there would be no verbal irony if the knowledge of the spectators were shared by the speaker, while some or all of the other characters were ignorant. This is, for instance, the case in Euripides' *Bacchae*, when the stranger says of the god: καὶ νῦν ἃ πάσχω πλη-

---

4. It is noteworthy that Kirkwood, after giving a workable definition, seems to ignore it himself. He says, for instance: 'There is a further irony in *Electra*, more essential to the tragedy than these two acts of deliberate deception: the irony of the situation of the sternly moral Electra, who is driven by her unflinching loyalty to the moral course of action into conduct which she herself recognizes as immoral' (259). This irony depends on interpretation, but apart from that: if Electra recognizes her own conduct as immoral, then she *is* aware of the 'true state of things'.

οἷον παρὼν ὁρᾷ, 'even now he is close by and sees what I suffer' (v. 500, transl. Kirk). Pentheus thinks that he is merely boasting; the chorus, though consisting of believers, do not know that the god is physically present in the shape of the stranger. The added meaning of this line, to which only the audience and the speaker himself are privy, is not 'contrary to the character's intention', as Pfister has it, but it does emphasize Pentheus' ignorance. When he answers that the god is not visible to his eyes (501), the effect is essentially the same. Both the statement of the knowing god and the reaction of his unwitting victim bring home to the audience that Pentheus is fatally blind to the truth. It is for this reason that I prefer not to exclude from the definition intentional extra meanings, and to describe the concept as follows: dramatic irony occurs as soon as the spectators know something that is unknown to at least one character on stage. The spectator's awareness of the ignorance of the character or characters may or may not be sharpened by verbal irony, occurring when an utterance is made that has an extra meaning not understood by the speaker himself and/or the listener or listeners on stage. A lie, told knowingly or unknowingly, may have the same effect.[5]

We would do well to keep in mind how vast the difference may be between a knowing and an unknowing spectator. How would a play-goer to whom even the name of Oedipus is unknown, experience the *Oedipus Tyrannus*? According to

---

5. This is, for instance, the case when Oedipus says he never saw Laius (v. 105). These words have, strictly speaking, no extra meaning, but they do sharpen the spectator's awareness of Oedipus' ignorance. They know that what he says is not true; he killed Laius, so he must have seen him.

Moles (90), such a spectator would remain ignorant until the *peripeteia*, but I do not think it would work quite this way. He will be ignorant indeed till the Tiresias scene, but by then all will depend on whether or not he believes the words of the seer. If he does, in the knowledge that, in tragedy at least, seers always speak the truth, he will know by vv. 350-3 that Oedipus is the murderer. But he will continue to be disturbed by the question of whether Oedipus, in denying the accusation, is being truthful. And if he is, how then is it possible that he murdered the king of Thebes without knowing it?

At the end of the Tiresias scene our imaginary spectator learns the whole truth: Oedipus is married to his mother and has murdered his father. He can infer now that this father must be Laius, but he still has no inkling of how all this could have happened. It is only during the second *epeisodion*, when Iocasta relates how and why her child was abandoned, and Oedipus reveals his own past, that he may be able to reconstruct the events.

Of course it is impossible to prove that an unknowing spectator will react in this way, but it is fairly certain that he will see the first half of the play as a kind of thriller. He will be preoccupied with such questions as: who did it, how did it happen and why? For the knowing spectator there is only one question: how will Oedipus find out? All the other issues have been clear from the beginning. This knowledge no doubt affects his state of mind, but it is difficult to say exactly how.

According to Markantonatos (98), dramatic irony 'implies an attitude of "detachment" on the part of the audience', and Sedgewick (13-14) concurs. Muecke puts it as follows: '...there is a special pleasure in seeing someone serenely unaware of being in a predicament' (63) and '...the ironic observer ... is detached from what he observes and this ironic spectacle has ... an aesthetic quality which, so to speak, objectifies it' (63-4). Johnson, on the other hand, does not seem to believe in this detachment: 'The dramatic interest is maintained *not*, as is sometimes said, by the sense of superiority of knowledge, but by the emotions which arise from that knowledge such as pity, fear or a sense of fun' (209).[6] Stanford's view is not entirely clear. He considers curiosity 'less emotive' than foreknowledge (1983, 19), but elsewhere he says of dramatic irony: 'Its range is restricted and it is mainly rational and analytical' and: 'There is usually an element of cool Olympian detachment in it...' (113). Since foreknowledge entails dramatic irony, I do not consider these statements compatible.

First of all we must remember that we never know for sure what goes on in the mind of the spectator. But I think it improbable that dramatic irony always produces the same effect. It undoubtedly operates differently according to the particular character who is acting in ignorance. There is a difference between watching the brutal tyrant Lycus enter the house where death awaits him, and seeing Iphigenia joyfully embrace her father, who is planning to kill her. It is hard to imagine a spectator watching both of them with the same degree of detachment or pleasure.

If we confine our discussion to the *Oedipus Tyrannus*, I am inclined to side with Johnson rather than with the other

---

6. Referring to 'a sense of fun', Johnson of course means comedy, not tragedy.

authors quoted above. It is true that, by virtue of their prior knowledge, the audience are detached, but detached from what? My answer would be: from the enigmas confronting an unknowing spectator. Their knowledge frees them from the obligation to try to solve these enigmas, and thus enables them to concentrate more intensely on Oedipus, and to sympathize more deeply with him.

However, the subject of this chapter is not the feelings provoked by dramatic irony, but rather the knowledge on which it is based. How do spectators acquire this knowledge? There are two main possibilities. In the first case, one or more characters are uninformed about something that has been said or done in a previous scene, while the spectators *are* aware of the foregoing words and actions. In the second case, the audience are familiar with the material - whatever its nature - which the author has used to create his plot. Of course, the two possibilities are not mutually exclusive. In the case of Sophocles' *Philoctetes*, for example, their knowledge of the myth told the audience that despite his fierce resistance, Philoctetes would go to Troy in the end. The prologue informed them of the schemes of Odysseus and Neoptolemus, so that during the subsequent scenes they knew that Philoctetes was the victim of deceit. But they did not know what would then follow. The myth determines the inevitable dénouement, but it is brought about in a quite unexpected fashion.

An additional possibility involves the title of a play. Even a theatre-goer who has never heard of the French Revolution will know that in a play entitled *Dantons Tod*, Danton will probably die. However, Greek tragedy provides no such examples. Ἡρακλῆς μαινόμενος might be a case in point, but when it was first produced the play was called simply Ἡρακλῆς. As Wilamowitz aptly observes: '...es wäre nicht bloss überflüssig, sondern störend gewesen, wenn Euripides hätte μαινόμενος zusetzen wollen: der ganze Herakles ist darin' (Zw. Band, 166).

Pfister (69) also adduces generic expectation ('Gattungs-erwartung') as a possible source of the audience's knowledge. When, for example, they see a character in comedy wrestling with difficulties, they may think: no matter how many prob-lems you have, I know that this is a comedy and that all will end well for you. Likewise, an audience may expect disaster simply because they know the play to be a tragedy. But cata-strophe was not inherent in Greek tragedy, and it is difficult to generalize on this point. Moreover, the mere knowledge that all will end badly does not enable the audience to understand that a character is fundamentally deluded. Thus generic expec-tation does not help them to understand that when Oedipus curses the murderer, he is cursing himself.

And finally, spectators may have seen or read the play beforehand. Of course, this would have been virtually impos-sible in fifth-century Athens, but even leaving that aside, it does not make sense to allow for this possibility. When the audience know a play, even a thriller that yields its secret only in the very last line is brimming with dramatic irony. To take another example, when today's audiences watch *Hamlet*, there is a fair chance that most of them have read or seen the play before. These spectators know, for instance, how Polonius will be killed by Hamlet, but it would make no sense to speak of dramatic irony here: this prior knowledge is not provided by the composition of the play, and when the play was first produced the death of Polonius was not an unvarying fact in a well-known tale. Here again, we must beware of the reader's viewpoint, and bear in mind the spectator to whom the play is new.

Many authors scarcely bother to ask what the audience knew. Markantonatos, for example, though most of his book is devoted to dramatic irony, touches on the question only briefly, and his argument is far from clear. 'The device of dramatic irony', he says, 'implies also an audience acquainted with the facts. It is well-known that the spectator in Greek theatre was usually familiar with the plot, because the subject matter of the play was taken from traditional legend or myth' (96). And on the same page we read that 'there were some cases in which the spectators could not all be expected to know even the minor details of a story'. Both statements are inaccurate. The spectator was not familiar with the *plot*, since traditional legend or myth might yield a number of plots. Nor could they ever know the minor details of a story, since only the broad outlines were fixed (cf. ch. 2). However, here at least, Markantonatos does not forget the audience, as he does when setting out his analysis of the ironies in Aeschylus' *Agamemnon*: 'In the following notes it will be presumed that the reader has the full text of the play in his mind or open before him. Otherwise many of the ambiguities, in which irony lies, will tend to seem abrupt and bald noted almost in isolation as here' (112). Here he is thinking of the reader who knows not only the plot but also the text of the play.

As I argued in ch. 2, it is not possible to make generalizations about the audience's knowledge. The story of Oedipus and of his sons must have been known, but what of his daughters at the time the *Antigone* was first produced? Some scholars are inclined to believe that the entire play is fictional. Others protest against this view, arguing that the main theme of the story already existed. But in all probability, it was not a well-known story, and even if the end of the *Seven* were authentic, and if part of Sophocles' audience had watched it, their prior knowledge is bound to have been minimal.

What *was*, then, the main theme of the story? Apparently, there was only one invariable fact: Antigone tries to bury Polynices despite a decree forbidding it.[7] All other features of Sophocles' play were floating details. Creon's part was not fixed, as is clear from the fact that, according to a dithyramb of Ion, Antigone was burned to death by Eteocles' son in a temple of Hera. Ion makes her suffer this fate together with Ismene, but Mimnermus relates that Ismene was killed by Tydeus, apparently before the storming of the town. Thus the part played by Ismene was not fixed either, nor that of Haemon, who in the *Oedipodeia* seems to have been a victim of the Sphinx. And finally, even Antigone's death was not one of the unvarying parts of the legend, since Euripides felt that it could be dropped from his play.[8] We may, therefore, con-

---

7. If, as many scholars assume, vv. 1744-6 of Euripides' *Phoenician Women* are indeed an interpolation, then in this play Antigone renounces even the attempt. For a dissenting opinion, see Saïd, 526.

8. See the *hypothesis* I and II of *Antigone*. Haemon's fate is mentioned in schol. Eur. *Phoen.* 1760, but the information may be unreliable since the

clude that the audience had nothing to go on at the beginning
of the play, and that, as Kamerbeek observes: '...“tragic irony”
in its strict sense (such as we encounter to so marked a degree
in the *Oedipus*) does not play an outstanding part in the
Antigone: the audience is not supposed to be aware beforehand
of the presuppositions of the dramatic action and its outcome...' (1978, 5).[9] When this tragic irony occurs, it is created by the composition of the play, not by prior knowledge of
the myth. I shall discuss a few examples.

During the prologue the audience learn that Antigone is set
on burying her brother despite Creon's edict and the death
penalty she risks. When the chorus make their entry, they still
know nothing, not even that Creon has forbidden Polynices'
burial. Their joy over the victory is unclouded, while the
audience realize that a new conflict is already brewing. When,
in the next *epeisodion*, Creon considers love of gain and
political machinations the only possible motives for the
offender, the spectators are acutely aware of his misconcep-
tion. No doubt their response to Creon's first appearance
would be different if Sophocles had chosen to withhold from

---

text of the scholium is clearly corrupt (see Davies, 20).

For a full discussion of the data, see for instance Kamerbeek (1978,
1-5), Müller (21-24) and Petersmann's article. Müller considers it probable
that Sophocles invented all the events of the play. Petersmann objects;
according to him the story of Antigone burying her brother already existed.
Kamerbeek observes that, even if it did, 'we may safely state that in the
Antigone the handling of the story and the building up of the conflict and
its outcome are as original as anything in Greek Tragedy' (5).

9. As will be clear from this quotation, Kamerbeek uses the term 'tragic
irony' in the same sense as dramatic irony.

them Antigone's plans. Bremer has even contended that the mere fact that Sophocles composed his tragedy in this way proves Hegel's interpretation to be wrong.[10]

There is one passage in Creon's text that has been singled out by several scholars as an instance of dramatic irony. It concerns vv. 184-6:

ἐγὼ γάρ, ἴστω Ζεὺς ὁ πάνθ' ὁρῶν ἀεί,
οὔτ' ἂν σιωπήσαιμι τὴν ἄτην ὁρῶν
στείχουσαν ἀστοῖς ἀντὶ τῆς σωτηρίας

'For I - be Zeus my witness, who sees all things always -
would not be silent if I saw ruin, instead of safety,
coming to the citizens...' (transl. Jebb)

Kamerbeek comments: 'Here, unmistakably, tragic irony is to be perceived and we should remember these words in the Teiresias-scene'. According to Markantonatos 'the audience see an ironical incongruity between what he (Creon) believes he is and what he himself is actually going to be shown' (1973, 492). Winnington-Ingram (123) asks: 'Does he really believe that to bury Polynices, to treat him as a *philos*, will bring *ate* upon the citizens (185)? (The irony here is obvious.)'

At what exact moment does Creon speak these lines? He has entered at v. 162, so he has not yet spoken half of the 58 lines which make up his opening speech. He has not yet touched upon the subject of the burial; the audience, of course, expect him to do so (see vv. 23-4), but they cannot know how he will justify his decree, nor how he will connect

---

10. (1971) 164. Cf. Heath 75.

it with the principles he professes. Thus one may well wonder just how ironical these lines were to them.

Kamerbeek's observation is somewhat vague. Is the irony also felt by spectators who do not know that a Tiresias scene will follow? Or do they realize only then that these lines were ironical? In the case of Markantonatos, it is clear that the reader's viewpoint is paramount, since an audience cannot possibly know how Creon is 'actually going to be shown'. They only know that Antigone will try to bury Polynices, but that knowledge hardly adds an extra meaning to *these* words of Creon. They may think: you are blind, for you do not understand that the decree you are going to issue is incompatible with your noble principles. And perhaps this is the very irony meant by Winnington-Ingram, though the question of whether Creon believes what he says is actually irrelevant. Sophocles has him say it, and there is no indication that he is not sincere.

If we assume that the audience reacted in the way I suggest, it is possible to speak of dramatic irony, though this is no longer verifiable. The assumption could be based on the spectators' superior judgment, but not on their superior knowledge. But *did* the Athenian spectators react this way? Here we are on slippery ground, as shown by the widely divergent opinions on the question of the extent to which Creon's decree was acceptable to the original audience (cf. ch. 5). It is not easy to assess with any certainty the Athenians' response to vv. 184-6, and for this reason I believe that the irony of these lines is less self-evident than the commentators assume.

When Antigone is brought in by the guard, the balance of information between characters and audience is restored.

Nevertheless, Di Virgilio (29) is convinced that there is a clear example of verbal irony in v. 575: he reads ἐμοί (with LF) and supposes that in this line Creon is unwittingly announcing the suicide of his wife Eurydice. At first sight, this would seem to be a typical reader's interpretation, since the audience have no reason to suppose that Creon's wife (who is first mentioned at v. 1180) is going to play any part at all. Yet Di Virgilio does not forget the spectators. He argues (29 n. 2) that the actor can bring home the irony by pointing ostentatiously to himself. However, I find it difficult to believe that on hearing a perfectly understandable statement, spectators would have been capable of grasping such a second meaning, which bears on the death of someone whose existence is not even known to them. If the actor did manage to impart this meaning, it must have been by a very broad hint indeed, at the expense of his character's credibility.

It has often been argued that, in the second stasimon in particular, the chorus are referring to Antigone, while Sophocles is referring to Creon and intends the audience to take it this way.[11] If we choose to call this irony, then again, as in

---

11. This is, for instance, the view of Müller, as well as of Winnington-Ingram: '...it is characteristic of the odes of this play that they tend, ironically, to carry a secondary reference to Creon which cannot be in the minds of the singers' (97); in n. 17: 'The choral use of dramatic irony is recognized and expounded by G. Müller...'. Kamerbeek: 'λόγου τ' ἄνοια καὶ φρενῶν Ἐρινύς (603) may be thought to refer to Antigone's stubbornness but not necessarily so. And this remark equally applies (or even still more cogently) to the whole second antistrophe, the ambivalence of which is such that a discerning hearer cannot but be reminded of Creon rather than of Antigone' (18).

the case of vv. 184-6, it is the result not of superior knowledge but of superior judgment. The chorus do know all the
facts, but their judgment of these facts is misguided while that
of the spectators is not. This irony is dependent on interpretation, but if there were no discrepancy between chorus and
audience, either in knowledge or in judgment, it would be
very hard to detect any irony. And yet, that is what Burton is
trying to do when he describes both the first and the second
stasimon as 'powerful instruments of dramatic irony' (136),
but nonetheless comments on the second: 'We should not
however be induced by romantic conceptions of what Antigone has done into believing that the ode cannot possibly refer
to her and must therefore refer to Creon. He has not yet done
or said anything that these elders could interpret as folly in
words and madness in the brain, though in the sequel it is he
who is going to be shown as the possessor of a mind deeply
and irrevocably impaired. Therein lies the irony which is
inherent to a greater or lesser extent in so many of Sophocles'
odes. At this stage of the play however our thoughts are
riveted upon Antigone and her deed; and the audience expects
that the song will offer some reflections on the extinction of
the house which that deed has ensured' (110-1). After the first
sentence of this quotation Burton refers to Müller, apparently
because he disagrees with his interpretation, and does *not*
think there is any discrepancy between chorus and audience.[12] But why then is the ode a 'powerful instrument of
dramatic irony'? Because Creon *in the sequel ...* is going to

12. Burton does not do justice to Müller's argument, since Müller does
not say that the *elders* refer to Creon but that Sophocles does.

be shown as the possessor of a mind deeply and irrevocably impaired'?

Elsewhere in his book, when discussing *Oedipus Tyrannus* 883-896, Burton observes: 'Nevertheless, there is in this stanza an ambiguity of language, probably intentional, which is essential to its irony, for when the truth comes out at the end of the play, it will be seen that Oedipus has, although unwittingly, in fact committed some of the sins here listed, above all parricide and incest which are so faintly suggested in 890 f. that the reference only becomes apparent in retrospect' (165).[13] From this passage I conclude that he would agree with Moles' statement: 'Irony of course can work retrospectively' (90 n. 2).[14] But how? Moles argues: 'In fact, if the ἔκπληξις felt by the audience at the ἀναγνώρισις of the *Oedipus* is of a detective-story kind, it is actually enhanced by the previous ironic effects, whose true meaning is only made clear by the ἀναγνώρισις itself' (ib.). However, in addition to the fact that an audience without prior knowledge will probably realize the truth in an earlier phase (see above pp. 73-4), one would be interested to know how this process works. I think it improbable that all verbal ironies again come to mind

---

13. If we assume that the audience knew the truth by virtue of their prior knowledge, the restriction in the final words of this quotation is of course superfluous. It is strange that the knowledge of the audience, here ignored, seems elsewhere self-evident to Burton. Cf. on p. 150: 'There is a terrible irony in this, as the Theban elders allow their imaginations to envisage the outcast's fate without knowing what the audience know, that this outcast is their king.'

14. Cf. Kirkwood: 'the effect of the prayer is, in retrospect, ironical in the extreme' (254-5).

once the knowledge needed to understand them has been gained. Since they go unnoticed at the time, there is no reason to assume that they are retained in the spectators' mind. It is true, of course, that having discovered the truth, they will reinterpret what they have witnessed; they will then realize that they have strayed in the fog together with Oedipus and that his energetic search was doomed to end in his ruin. But let us again imagine a real thriller. In the very last scene the young man we liked so much throughout the play proves to be a brutal murderer. No doubt we will, in retrospect, reinterpret his behaviour, but we have watched in ignorance and our reactions *during* the play would have been quite different if we had known the truth from the beginning. If we speak of dramatic irony in both cases, the term acquires a range which is so broad that it ceases to be meaningful.

When Antigone reappears there is again dramatic irony, albeit of an unusual kind, which remains until she departs to meet her death. The chorus, though trying to console her, do not confirm that she has done the right thing in burying Polynices and that her death is undeserved. In this way they create, as von Fritz puts it, 'jene ungeheure Einsamkeit um Antigone' (239). She thinks that she will die ἄκλαυτος, ἄφιλος (v. 876); she does not know that Haemon and the citizens of Thebes side with her and admire her. But the audience, like the chorus, *do* know; they possess the knowledge that could ease her journey to the dark chamber. It is noteworthy that Antigone is to die without this knowledge. Szlezák (9) rightly notes that an intrinsic quality of dramatic irony is that it comes to an end. Characters always come to know, if only in the face of death, what the audience knew already. Antigone is an exception. To my knowledge the only other one is Xuthus at the end of Euripides' *Ion*; he goes back to Athens happily convinced that he is taking with him his son, while all other characters and the audience know that Ion is the son of Apollo.

The most intriguing problem concerning dramatic irony in the *Antigone* is raised by the fifth stasimon. The ode is often compared to the third stasimon of the *Oedipus Tyrannus* since 'this stasimon also breathes a spirit of almost ecstatic hope and faith that all will end well' (Kamerbeek 1978, 25); and it does so just before the catastrophe occurs. Winnington-Ingram comments: '...perhaps it is the irony of the Chorus' prayer which is most salient. What takes place, what the Messenger relates, is an outbreak of pathological violence which it would be vain to hope that Dionysus would cure, since it springs from mad emotion' (115). Gardiner also mentions 'the pungent irony of the song' (95) and on the same page she speaks of 'an event which the audience fully expects - the report of disaster -'. But *did* they expect this and did they, as a consequence, feel the irony while the ode was sung?

Jebb considered it a blemish of the play that Antigone could have been saved if Creon had not chosen, for some inexplicable reason, to bury Polynices first: 'A fatal delay must not seem to be the result merely of negligence or of caprice' (xix). Later commentators have disposed of this argument: the point of no return is reached at vv. 1064-7. Tiresias' announcement is unconditional[15] and since Hae-

---

15. See, for instance, Müller: 'das von nun an unabwendbare Unheil, Haimons Tod' (231).

mon's death is tied up with Antigone's, Creon would have come too late anyway.[16]

Jebb's censure is, indeed, unjustified, but what may an audience expect after Tiresias' prophecy? He foretells Haemon's death and announces that there will be laments of - or about - men and women in the palace (1078-9). But he says nothing about Antigone's fate, let alone about Eurydice, whose existence is as yet unknown to the spectators. They cannot, therefore, really expect 'an outbreak of pathological violence'. They can at most foresee, in view of v. 751, that Haemon will commit suicide.

There is, however, more. Tiresias' announcement may be unconditional but neither the chorus nor Creon notice this. They are shocked and frightened by it, but they think there is still time to repair things. And if the spectators were indeed convinced that Haemon would die, while the characters were not, this superior knowledge would come about in a curious way. Audience and characters hear the same words and - here the scene differs from the Tiresias scene in the *Oedipus Tyrannus* - both groups believe these words to be true. But only

---

16. Gardiner argues that it is not even true that Creon postpones Antigone's deliverance till after Polynices' burial: '...it is likely that when Creon orders servants to fetch axes and go "yonder", adding that he himself will be present to free her (1108-1112), some members of his retinue are meant to exit at once. The audience would suppose that they are going on ahead to begin the task of opening the tomb with tools. As one listens to the Messenger's speech, one perceives that Creon assumed the tomb would be opened by the time he got there...' (94-95 n. 21). She may well be right, but I do not think that the sequence of Creon's actions is really important.

the audience would realize the full meaning of what they were hearing. Generic expectation may be involved here. As I said above, catastrophic endings are not inherent in Greek tragedy, but experienced Athenian theatre-goers may have sensed at this stage of the tragedy that a happy ending was no longer possible.

It may have worked this way, but I am not sure. I do think it possible that at least part of the audience took it for granted, as did Creon and the chorus, that the condition ('if you do not bury Polynices and free Antigone'), though not explicitly stated, was implied in Tiresias' words. If they did, they may have been carried away by the prayer and may have shared the chorus' hope, until they realized, in retrospect, that the hope had been vain and that the prophecy had never allowed for any escape.[17] In this case their emotional response during the song was not coloured by dramatic irony, and the effect of the ode must have been quite different from that of the third stasimon of the *Oedipus Tyrannus* on the audience. This does not mean that the comparison is ill-founded. In both cases an outburst of hopeful expectation precedes the disaster. But the impact on the spectators' minds may have been different.

So much for the examples drawn from the *Antigone*. Since there is no sense in presenting an endless list of comparable cases, I shall confine myself to a few more examples from

---

17. Kamerbeek comments: 'But although the hearer knows that Teiresias' prophesies will be fulfilled, he will for the moment be swept along by the joyous dance-song and be misled into illusory hope against his better knowledge' (25). However, this too is no more than a guess.

other plays. I have chosen Sophocles' *Trachinian Women* and Euripides' *Heracles*, because the myths surrounding Heracles' career are so numerous and diverse that it is difficult to reconstruct the audience's knowledge and expectations. As a result, these tragedies - in particular *Heracles* - present a number of specific problems.

In her edition of the *Trachinian Women*, Easterling argues that the story of the capture of Oechalia to obtain Iole, and the story of the poisoned robe were probably well-known (15). There was, however, no fixed relationship between them: in *Heracles*, for instance, the destruction of Oechalia is already part of the past (see vv. 472-3) and is not linked to Heracles' death. I assume, therefore, that Sophocles' audience, upon learning of Heracles' siege of the town (vv. 74-5), had no immediate reason to assume that the play would be about Heracles' death by the poisoned robe. On the other hand, the prophecy quoted by Deianira (vv. 79-81) may have steered their expectations in this direction, since they knew that a calm and happy life was not in store for Heracles. Moreover, the prologue makes it clear that Deianira has adult sons, and only one story was connected with this phase of her married life: the story of the robe that ended the marriage. Perhaps the spectators allowed for the possibility that the plot was invented by Sophocles, but all in all, I think it probable that at the end of the prologue they were able to guess the theme of the play.

If this is true, then most of the ironies pointed out by commentators must have been perceived by the audience. Easterling, for instance, comments on vv. 92-3: 'There is irony in these words for anyone who knows from the story what kind of news Hyllus will in fact hear'. Strictly speaking, the audience cannot know what Hyllus will hear, since they have only been told that Heracles is making war upon Oechalia or is planning to do so (vv. 74-5). They have not been told that the town has already been captured, and the robe has not yet been sent. However, Easterling is quite right in connecting the irony of these lines with the audience's foreknowledge.

Here, as elsewhere,[18] Easterling seems to allow for two kinds of reactions, those of the knowing and those of the unknowing spectator. But in her comment on Lichas' speech (vv. 248-90) she says that 'the audience has no reason to disbelieve him', though there is a 'disturbing uneasiness in Lichas' tone'. And yet, the capture of Oechalia was traditionally linked with Heracles' passion for Iole and if all or part of the audience were familiar with this tradition, then they did have reason to disbelieve Lichas. If they did not know of it, they may have sensed that he was hiding something, always provided that there was uneasiness in the actor's tone; the words in themselves do not really give rise to suspicion. There is in Lichas' speech either dramatic irony or preparation for new information.

Another case in point is vv. 180-204; as Easterling observes, 'This is the only moment of unclouded joy in the play,

---

18. Cf., for instance, her comment on 492-5: 'Soph. gives no hint at this stage that D. is planning to use magic, and there is certain an element of surprise at the beginning of the next episode (531ff.), when she announces that she cannot endure Iole as a rival in her own house. But a spectator or reader familiar with the myth might sense an unintentionally ominous note in her words ἀντὶ δώρων δῶρα and particularly προσαρμόσαι "adjust", "make fit", in view of the story of the fatally clinging robe'.

though even here the ironical echoes of the Parodos may cast a shadow for the audience'. In the light of her comment on vv. 200-4, Easterling is apparently thinking here of Deianira's joy recalling the cycle of joy and sorrow which is a main theme in the Parodos. The chorus is convinced that, for Heracles, the circle has come round to joy, while Deianira, too, believes for a brief moment that there will be happiness at last. However, the joy of spectators who know the story can never be unclouded, with or without ironical echoes. And one may well ask whether spectators without prior knowledge are able to detect the irony in the Parodos. Here again one may allow for generic expectation but, as I maintained above, it is plausible that the audience did possess prior knowledge and understood what would happen as a result of the capture of Oechalia.

In Euripides' *Heracles* things are more complicated. The story of Lycus was probably the poet's own invention, as was Theseus' appearance. The murder of the children was not, but chronologically it seems to have come before the twelve labours.[19] Moreover, since Pindar (*Isth.* 3/4, 79-81) ignores the tale of the murder and makes Heracles' sons die in armour, it was apparently not one of the basic facts of the myth.

What could the audience expect during the first part of the play? When confronted with a situation which they did not know from mythology, the audience may have expected that all of the play was invention, and that the revenge on Lycus would be its main theme. They probably guessed that revenge

---

19. See the Introduction of Bond's commentary.

would be taken, as Heracles' return from the nether world was a basic fact of his myth. They could not know for sure whether he would come in time to save his family. But they probably expected this to happen, since, as Michelini (241) argues, 'the device of suppliancy presupposes some sort of rescue, the choice of letting the suppliants die is no real choice at all'. When he does indeed arrive in time, quite early in the play, and there seems to be nothing standing in the way of the revenge, the audience may well have sensed that more sweeping events would follow. Did they, by then, expect that after saving his children, Heracles would then kill them? Or did they expect something new and surprising invented by Euripides, as in the case of the Lycus episode? It is impossible to answer these questions, especially since it is difficult to assess whether the infanticide was already a well-known feature of the Heracles myth. If it was, the audience may have expected it to occur later on in the play. We cannot, I think, go beyond that.

In his article on the *Heracles* Kamerbeek shows himself very much aware of these uncertainties, but nevertheless he argues: 'The possibility, however, of "tragic irony" (and therewith of a strong interrelation between the first part and the rest) remains (1) because the poet at all events knows what he is after, (2) because - in my opinion - the events, the spectacles, the utterances in the first part of a play have to be seen in the light of what follows as well as the reverse. And although it is true that in a sense the poet has done his utmost to render the second reversal of fortune as sudden and bewildering as possible, there are some details in part I which would seem to make the attentive hearer pause - not as an afterthought but even before the central event, even without any knowledge of the terrible things to come, whereas there are a great number of them which only become meaningful after the event - indeed, I do not hesitate to assert that the whole of part I yields its full meaning only when seen in the light which the subsequent parts are to shed on it' (5).

I find this somewhat confusing. It goes without saying that the poet knows what he is after, and that we must view the play as a whole; this holds true for all tragedies. But dramatic irony has to do not with the knowledge of the poet, but with the experience of the spectator who is watching the play. When this spectator does not even know the story of the child-murder, he will at most feel a premonition of impending disaster. But such a feeling does not enable an audience to detect verbal ironies, or to foresee that a word or a scene will be echoed in a later phase of the play.[20]

Let us turn for a moment to some of Kamerbeek's examples. He agrees with Wilamowitz that 'the spectacle of Heracles taking in tow his children when he enters his house finds its counterpart in Heracles following Theseus, πανώλεις ἐφολκίδες, at the end of the play, with the corpses of the children and Megara in the background' (5). This is true, of course, and the actor, knowing what will come, will see to it that the impact of Heracles' exit with the children is such that the audience cannot fail to remember it at the close of the play. I even suspect that Euripides has added the simile in v. 632 to make the metaphor ἐφολκίδας (631) sink in, so that it

---

20. Kamerbeek does not make it clear which details in part I 'would seem to make the attentive hearer pause'.

would be remembered when Heracles speaks v. 1424.[21] But no spectator could possibly guess that at the end of the tragedy Heracles would leave the stage in Theseus' wake. When he does, the spectators will remember his former exit, which only then acquires its full meaning. While at the time it may be ironic, if the audience know that Heracles will later kill his children, it cannot be seen as ironic in relationship to the Theseus scene.

Ironies, says Kamerbeek, 'are to be heard in Megara's words (fifty lines before Heracles' arrival) where she describes how Heracles wanted to bequeath his inheritance to his sons: ἐς δεξιάν τε σὴν ἀλεξητήριον / ξύλον κ α θ ί ε ι δαίδα-λον, ψευδῆ δόσιν (470, 1); cp. in the Messenger's speech ὑπὲρ κάρα βαλὼν / ξύλον καθῆκε παιδὸς ἐς ξανθὸν κάρα, / ἔρρηξε δ' ὀστᾶ (992-94)' (6). Here, indeed, is a verbal reminiscence that seems to be intended to send the spectator's mind back to Megara's description of Heracles playing with his children. It heightens the horror of the boy's death, but it cannot lend irony to Megara's words. There can only be irony at vv. 470-1 if the hearers already expect not Lycus but Heracles to kill the children, and if they are aware of the contrast, as yet unknown to Megara, between the loving father and the mad child-murderer.

---

21. Of course, the added simile also has a function in the immediate context. Michelini (253 n. 100) aptly observes: 'A difference between the two occurrences is that at line 632 the metaphor is glossed ... presumably a touch aimed at the children, who will like the image and who will also need to have it explained'.

Finally we come to a problem from this same tragedy, which is discussed by Bremer in his article on v. 581. Though he does not use the term dramatic irony, it may be interesting to look at it in this light. Referring to the words τῶν δ' ἐμῶν τέκνων οὐκ ἐκπονήσω θάνατον, Bremer argues that the normal meaning of ἐκπονεῖν was 'to accomplish' and that the audience could only interpret it as 'to shield off', because the context led them to understand it that way. Meanwhile, however, the usual meaning had done its work. Euripides 'wants to bring the public into a momentary state of being puzzled; presently they are helped out of this perplexity by the immediate context ('of course ἐκπονήσω *must* mean πόνῳ κωλύσω'), but subconsciously their first understanding perseveres, and so their mind is prepared for what is to follow...' (240). Bond, in his commentary on the play, agrees that ἐκπονεῖν cannot mean 'labour to avert', but thinks it possible to render the words as follows: 'Will I not exert myself over my children's mortal danger?'. Nonetheless, he accepts the possibility of an ambiguity, though he considers it improbable that the meaning 'to accomplish' struck the audience first: '...have they really time to think it over and make the necessary adjustment?' (211 n. 2). However, I do not think this objection is valid. The actor can give them time by a slight pause after the rhetorical question.

If we assume that the audience did indeed, for a moment, interpret Heracles' words as 'shall I not accomplish the death of my own children?', how then were they affected by it? According to Bremer, they were prepared for what was to follow. But if they were already expecting the murder of the children, the double meaning may have confirmed their expectation. It is even conceivable that the sentence worked as an eye-opener: so that is what is going to happen! In both cases it is possible to speak of 'preparation by announcement', but Heracles makes the announcement unwittingly and it is not understood by the characters. So there is, at the same time, verbal dramatic irony.

The discussions in this chapter lead me to the following general conclusions:
- Irony is a complex phenomenon, but for this very reason it is best to define it.
- In principle, dramatic irony as defined above (p. 73) is verifiable, but we cannot always be sure about the audience's prior knowledge.
- When the audience do not know more than the characters, they may yet surpass them in the soundness of their judgment. In such cases dramatic irony will depend on interpretation.
- 'Dramatic irony in retrospect' is a kind of *contradictio in terminis* and ought to be known by some other term.

5. THE RESPONSE OF THE AUDIENCE

As I maintained in the previous chapter, it is not always easy to assess what the Athenian audience knew and expected. It is even more difficult to venture an opinion on their emotional response, or indeed on that of any audience. And yet, it is remarkable how readily observations on this subject are made. For a number of scholars the workings of the audience's mind seem to harbour no secrets.

We will turn again to the subject of foreknowledge. In his book *The Rhetoric of Fiction* Booth asserts: '...unless the work gains in dramatic irony for each loss in mere mystery, second reading will be disappointing' (285). Though he is referring to the reading of novels, I suspect that he would say the same of the seeing of plays. Of course, no two performances are ever exactly the same, and even when we have seen or read a play several times, a new production may open up unknown vistas. But we know what will happen and what will be said, and nevertheless it is possible to enjoy a play again and again. Does this enjoyment result, as Booth will have it, from our all-embracing knowledge?

Pütz puts forward another explanation: 'Wir alle kennen die Empfindungen, wenn wir "Wallenstein" oder "Hamlet" zu wiederholten Malen sehen oder lesen. Wie die Zuschauer des Passionsspiels warten wir mit höchster Anspannung auf Leiden und Tod der Hauptperson. Es scheint fast so, als gingen wir auf das Spiel ein, indem wir uns in den Stand der Unwissenheit zurückversetzten' (14). Is this what happens to us when we see a play that we know through and through?

Views similar to those of Pütz have been expressed with respect to spectators who already know the basic facts of the myth. In his last book Stanford argues: 'If the acting and the language are compelling enough an audience may forget its foreknowledge and live by empathy in the present moment of the play' (144). Markantonatos, speaking of the *Oedipus Tyrannus*, asserts: '...when the prophet Teiresias detects the awful truth and alludes openly to Oedipus' incest (366-7), the spectators, though knowing that what Teiresias says is quite true, have so identified themselves with Oedipus that their sympathy makes them deaf to the seer's utterances. Thus knowledge yields to feeling' (236). This view is much like that of Webster, who says of the same scene: 'Knowledge yields to feeling and the spectator identifies himself with Oedipus' (118). Webster is also convinced that, in Sophocles' *Electra*, the audience really believe that Orestes is dead: 'The audience know the truth, but they have so identified themselves with the chief character that their sympathy leads them to disbelieve what they know to be true' (ib.). Lucas says in this respect: 'Though few go so far as to forget that they are in a theatre, we do in a sense suspend our knowledge when we put ourselves sympathetically in the position of those who do not possess that knowledge. Otherwise we should rarely want to see a play, or to read a novel, twice' (133, ad 1452 b 7). And finally we have Knox, who says of Oedipus: 'So deeply do we desire to see him escape that we are momentarily caught up in the mad enthusiasm of his most confident declaration: "I count myself the son of Chance, the giver of good"' and, on the third stasimon: 'the chorus ... is hoping for a miracle that will save Oedipus from destruction, and that is how we feel too' (1957, 51).[1]

It is not my aim to challenge the views presented in this modest anthology. I am, however, amazed at the confidence with which these statements are made. The authors quoted above appear to be so certain about the feelings of 'the' audience that they do not even take the trouble to explain how they know all this.[2] Such knowledge can perhaps be attained by extensive audience research, a kind of research which is complicated, time-consuming and beset with methodical problems, as the work of scholars in this field makes abundantly clear.[3] If the classical scholars I mentioned had done

---

1. I do not quite understand why the chorus would fear the *destruction* of Oedipus. They cannot guess what will follow; they only know that Oedipus may be the murderer of Laius. But nothing in the text suggests that, at this moment, the murder is foremost in their mind.

2. Lucas is the only author who clarifies his argument: 'Otherwise we should rarely want to see a play, or to read a novel, twice'. But this is not decisive, in view of Booth's conflicting opinion.

3. These scholars are now united in the ICRAR (International Committee for Reception and Audience Research). Sauter, editor of *New Directions in Audience Research* (1988), opens his Introductory Notes as follows: '"Who experiences what in a theatrical performance, and why?" asked Zagorski in

such research, they surely would have reported on it. As it is, I suspect that their views reflect their personal experience, and I can only say that this experience is different from mine. My memory may deceive me, since it is difficult enough to reconstruct one's own reactions, but I remember weeping during Electra's lament, without for a moment believing that Orestes was really dead, and sympathizing with Oedipus without ever forgetting what I knew.

A dissenting view is put forward by Mathiessen: 'Nachdem Orestes im Prolog aufgetreten ist und den Botentrug angekündigt hat, wird auch ein noch so wirkungsvoller Botenbericht den Zuschauer in keinem Augenblick vergessen lassen, daß Orestes lebt und daß die Rachetat nahe bevorsteht' (116 n. 2). Admittedly, Mathiessen likewise fails to support his argument, but it cannot be denied that *his* view is the more plausible one. Sophocles has organized his tragedy in such a way that the audience learn, right at the beginning, that Orestes is alive and present. The spectators clearly know this, and when Webster claims that they then *en masse* disbelieve what they know, the burden of proof lies with him.

There is one more point which these experts on the mind of the audience fail to explain. According to Knox the spectators are 'momentarily caught up' in Oedipus' enthusiasm, but Markantonatos and Webster do not specify at what moment knowledge returns, once it has yielded to feeling. Or does it retreat altogether? In which case the dramatic irony is lost as well. Speculating on such questions may be an exciting pas-

---

an article in the Russian periodical *Life of the Art*. This was back in 1925 ... Today, more than 60 years later, this question is still valid' (5).

time, but we must beware of presenting speculations as facts, without even allowing for the possibility that different people may react in different ways.

When ascribing reactions to the Athenian audience, authors generally make use of arguments from history and literature. Nonetheless, it is difficult to obtain anything approaching solid evidence. No matter how much we know about Athenian society, it is far from easy to reconstruct the thoughts and feelings of its citizens. This is abundantly clear from the differing views on *Antigone* touched upon in the previous chapter. According to Calder, Creon's behaviour was essentially quite acceptable to the audience: 'His decree was severe, but it was wartime. His reaction to disobedience was adherence to the law. What else was feasible?' (403). Rösler, on the other hand argues: 'Kreons totale, kompromißlose Weigerung, den Leichnam des Polyneikes zur Bestattung freizugeben, stellte im Horizont des 5. Jh. keine überhaupt nur diskutable Reaktion auf dessen Verhalten dar...' (14); and, on the next page: 'Wenn Kreon gleich zu Beginn dem Chor zu verstehen gibt, er habe ihn wegen seines erprobten Gehorsams "von allem Volk gesondert" herberufen, oder wenn er wenig später von Reaktionen auf sein Regime berichtet: "Doch weil dies schon lange Männern / der Stadt ein Ärgernis ist, murren sie gegen mich, / die Häupter schüttelnd insgeheim, und wolln den Nacken / nicht halten unterm Joch, wie sich's gebührt", so ergab sich für das attische Publikum im Dionysos-Theater ein scharfer, unüberhörbarer Kontrast zu dem politischen System, in dem es selber lebte und mit dem es sich identifizierte'. Knox voices yet another view. Antigone, so he says, 'completely ignores the obligations which membership in the *polis* imposes, and even though Creon, their self-appointed spokes-man, is wrong in the demand he makes, those obligations exist and no one in the audience for whom the play was written would have denied their force or sympathized with Antigone's refusal to reckon with them' (1964, 114).[4]

These clearly represent three different reconstructions of the Athenians' response to the *Antigone*. Athenian society is apparently an ambiguous phenomenon, and the historical evidence may give rise to quite divergent opinions on the reactions of the Athenian audience. This must put us on our guard. Moreover, the world within the play cannot be equated with the world outside. This is in effect what Calder is doing when he says that it was 'wartime'. In real life, it would still be wartime if the enemy had fled only the night before, and if a treaty had not yet been made. But in the play, the danger is clearly over; the fact that strictly speaking the war has not yet ended is never presented as a factor of any importance. More-over, the prevailing views of an audience do not necessarily constitute the meaning of a play. Even if we knew for certain that most Athenians considered it quite acceptable to leave a traitor's corpse to the dogs, this would not prove that Sophocles meant them to side with Creon or that they actually did so. As Heath puts it: '...we are dealing here, not with an

---

4. The most ambitious endeavour to shed light on the *Antigone* by reconstructing the Athenians' world-view is that of Oudemans and Lardinois, who contrast our own 'separative cosmology' with the 'inter-connective cosmology' of the Greeks. However, this endeavour fails, in my opinion, as the authors' reasoning is often unsound and the book contains a number of outright contradictions.

Athenian court of law, but with a tragedy; whenever the refusal of burial becomes an issue in tragedy, it is seen as an emotive wrong...' (75).

Another example is to be found in a much-quoted observation from Dodds' commentary on Euripides' *Bacchae*. It concerns the words of Dionysus when Pentheus is about to leave for the Cithaeron (973-6):

ἔκτειν', Ἀγαύη, χεῖρας αἵ θ' ὁμόσποροι
Κάδμου θυγατέρες· τὸν νεανίαν ἄγω
τόνδ' εἰς ἀγῶνα μέγαν, ὁ νικήσων δ' ἐγὼ
καὶ Βρόμιος ἔσται. τἄλλα δ' αὐτὸ σημανεῖ.

'Stretch out your arms, Agaue, and you her sisters,
daughters of Cadmus; I am leading the youth
to his great contest - and the winner shall be I
and Bromios! The rest, the event itself will show.' (transl. Kirk)

Dodds comments: 'Mr. D.W. Lucas has called my attention to the significance of the description of Pentheus here as τὸν νεανίαν. He is in fact hardly more than a boy, as we may infer from 1185-7; and that is the one plea which a Greek audience would accept in extenuation of his conduct. The Greeks were very susceptible to the pathos inherent in the rashness of inexperienced youth: cf. e.g. *Odyssey* 7.294 αἰεὶ γάρ τε νεώτεροι ἀφραδέουσιν, Eur. *Supp.* 580 γνώσῃ σὺ πάσχων· νῦν δ' ἔτ' εἶ νεανίας, *IA.* 489 ἄφρων νέος τ' ἦ, fr.trag.adesp. 538 τὸ νέον ἅπαν ὑψηλόν ἐστι καὶ θρασύ, and Aristotle's characterization of young men at *Rhet.* 2.12, especially 1389 b 7 τὰ ἀδικήματα ἀδικοῦσιν εἰς ὕβριν καὶ οὐ κακουργίαν. I think Mr. Lucas is right in seeing here a first preparation for the shift of sympathy which the next two scenes will bring about'. Jeanne Roux, too, is convinced that Pentheus' youth propitiated the audience: 'Il appartient donc à la catégorie des héros jeunes, blonds et imberbes, Thésée, Achille, Pollux, Parthénopeus, tels qu'on se les représentait à l'époque des *Bacchantes*. ... Cette extrême jeunesse est essentielle dans le déroulement du drama. Elle devait *a priori* rendre le personnage sympathique au public' (*Introduction* 22-23). But can we really be sure of this?

Let us turn to the parallel passages referred to by Dodds, starting with *Rhetorics* 2.12. Aristotle argues that the orator, when confronted with youthful hearers, must be able to attune his speech to them. With this in mind, he describes the disposition of youthful males. They are, according to Aristotle, passionate and ambitious; their character is honest since they have not yet met with evil. They are trusting rather than calculating, and are easily deceived. Their behaviour is often intemperate, since they think they know everything. 'And their wrongful acts they perform out of excessiveness, not out of malice'.

Aristotle no doubt implies what Dodds explicitly states: young people deserve some measure of clemency. But this is the view of a philosopher, and we cannot possibly know whether it coincided with the *communis opinio* of his citizens, let alone with the common view of the Athenians who, some 75 years earlier, saw the first production of Euripides' play.[5]

---

5. Dodds speaks, rather sweepingly, of 'a Greek audience' and 'the Greeks'. But I assume that he is thinking first and foremost of the audience that saw the first production of the *Bacchae* in 405 BC.

Attic comedy suggests that time may indeed have been a factor here. According to Sommerstein 'Old Comedy, in marked contrast to New, throughout displays a systematic bias in favour of older and against younger men' (320; cf. Henderson 109). Any attempt at generalization which is based on Aristotle's opinion may well go astray.

The other passages likewise fail to support Dodds' argument, though for other reasons. While in all of them the behaviour of youth is censured, youth is never seen as a mitigating factor. Odysseus (η 294) praises Nausicaa, since she is the exception which proves the rule. The isolated *fr.adesp.* 538 states, in a somewhat generalising manner, that all young people are haughty and rash.[6] The herald in Euripides' *Suppliant Women* scoffs at Theseus' lack of experience.[7] In the *Iphigenia in Aulis*, when Menelaus uses the adjective νέος, he is censuring his own behaviour. A similar example is to be found in *Alcestis* 679-80, where Pheres hurls at Admetus the words:

ἄγαν ὑβρίζεις, καὶ νεανίας λόγους
ῥίπτων ἐς ἡμᾶς οὐ βαλὼν οὕτως ἄπει.

'Your insults go too far and you'll not get away
with hurling these brash taunts at me.' (transl. Conacher)

---

6. In the edition of Kannicht/Snell the line quoted by Dodds is no longer considered a fragment from tragedy.

7. My explanation of the word in *Suppl.* 580 is somewhat different from that of Collard, who renders it as 'headstrong'. In any case, the herald's tone is definitely aggressive.

Here, as in *Iphigenia in Aulis* 489, an adult is denounced: by using the word νεανίας, in this case as an adjective, Pheres makes clear that Admetus' words deserve blame. Still another example is Euripides' *Andromache* 184-5:

κακόν γε θνητοῖς τὸ νέον ἔν τε τῷ νέῳ
τὸ μὴ δίκαιον ὅστις ἀνθρώπων ἔχει.

'Youth is an evil for mankind, and in particular
when people in their youth are given to injustice.'

Hermione, to whom these words are addressed, is indeed young, but her youth is decidedly not seen as an excuse.

A distaste for youthful behaviour is reflected in all these quotations. We may even assume that they voice a common opinion, since otherwise νεανίας and νέος could not be used as they are in *Alcestis* 679 and *Iphigenia in Aulis* 489.[8] But nowhere is a plea for clemency made. Strangely enough, Dodds has overlooked *Hippolytus* 117-120, where such a plea *is* made. When Hippolytus, after a disparaging reference to Aphrodite, has left the stage, his old servant prays to the goddess, excusing his master's behaviour:

χρή δὲ συγγνώμην ἔχειν.
εἴ τις σ' ὑφ' ἥβης σπλάγχνον ἔντονον φέρων
μάταια βάζει, μὴ δόκει τούτου κλύειν·
σοφωτέρους γὰρ χρὴ βροτῶν εἶναι θέους.

'and one should be forgiving.
If one whose heart is vehement with youth
speaks idly of thee, pretend not to hear it:

---

8. A literal translation ('I was young'; 'youthful words') would not yield the necessary connotation in English.

gods should have greater wisdom than do men.' (transl. Barrett)

Here indeed the goddess is asked to indulge 'the rashness of inexperienced youth', and even the offence is comparable: both Pentheus and Hippolytus oppose a god.

However, the words of a stage-character do not tell us anything about the general opinion of an audience, even if they are in accordance with the author's intention. Euripides may well have wished that his audience felt as his character did, but we cannot know whether the servant's plea appealed to prevailing sentiments. It is equally possible that his prayer expressed a way of thinking that was *not* familiar to the audience.

Apart from Aristotle, Dodd's references are irrelevant as regards content. And even if they were not, statements from tragedies or epics do not necessarily express what 'the' Athenians felt. While I cannot actually prove him wrong, I feel that he is presenting as fact what is at most a guess. And he does so again when speaking of 'the shift of sympathy which the next two scenes will bring about'.

These words imply that the sympathy, till this moment, has been wholly on the side of the god. But whose sympathy? Dodds does not make this clear, but he is probably thinking again of the Athenian audience, or even perhaps of spectators in general. In any case, he informs us of their reactions as if there can be no doubt about the truth of his view. Stanford is of the same opinion, but his wording is somewhat different: 'In the first three-quarters of the play we are clearly intended to dislike Pentheus as a bullying puritan, and to sympathize with the debonair Dionysos. But our feelings must change when the Messenger (1115ff.) describes how the young king died...' (1983, 118). Here the 'shift of sympathy' is not presented as a fact, but as a kind of precept. 'We are clearly intended...' means: people who react otherwise fail to understand the tragedy in the right way.

The emotional response postulated by Dodds and Stanford has little to do with the reactions of a real audience, and everything to do with their own interpretation of the tragedy. This is the response which, in their view, Euripides intended; it is the response of the ideal spectator - ideal, that is, in their eyes. Since my view of the play is different, I do not agree with them. I cannot believe, for instance, that there is no sympathy and compassion for Pentheus when the stranger explicitly states that he will die, 'slaughtered by the hands of his mother' (vv. 857-9, not commented on by Dodds). From that moment on, even spectators without any prior knowledge are aware that Pentheus is doomed to die a gruesome death. Is it plausible that they should remain unmoved until the moment they hear that he has indeed been slaughtered? It is, however, not my intention to discuss the feelings which, in my view, the play should produce. I am merely pointing out the difference between the real spectator and the ideal spectator, who is in effect the reflection of our own interpretation.

It seems somewhat presumptuous to make a pronouncement on the feelings of 'the' audience, regardless of the time and society they live in, and the production they are watching. Even if producers are faithful to the text, they can stage a play in many different ways, each of which will affect the audience differently. Moreover, an audience is not a monolithic bloc. Spectators differ in intelligence and sensitivity. They may be open to a producer's interpretation when the play is new to them, but not when they know it, and have already formed their own opinion. As regards the Athenian audience of 405 B.C., they were certainly not automatically of one mind. But the play was new to all of them and they shared a social and religious background which, up to a point, can be reconstructed. Nevertheless there is no evidence which enables us to establish during which part of the play the Athenians began to sympathize with Pentheus.

The ideal spectator is, as I maintained above, the reflection of an interpretation. Dodds' phrase 'the shift of sympathy which the next two scenes will bring about' really means: the shift of sympathy which will occur when the audience react as I believe that Euripides intended. It is a figure of speech, presenting a personal view as an objective truth. Or, to quote Heath: it is the answer to an '*interpretative* question: what effect was this text *meant* to have?' (31)

Kirk (ad v. 974) objects to Dodds' comment for other reasons: 'It has been maintained by some critics that the description of Pentheus as a "youth" prepares the audience for a shift of sympathy toward him in the scenes that follow. This is improbable: "the youth" bears some emphasis, but not so much as would be needed to give this neutral word a definitely sympathetic colouring'.[9] Kirk does not enter into the problem of whether the Athenians considered Pentheus' youth an excuse for his behaviour; he only denies that the word νεα-νίαν can bear so much weight as Dodds will have it. This,

---

9. Kirk does not mention Dodds' name, but it is clear that he is referring to him.

however, is an irrelevant discussion, since both Kirk and Dodds are forgetting that the spectators had eyes of their own. Pentheus' youth, indicated in the text, was clearly shown by his mask. If his youth really appealed to the clemency of the audience, this must have been the case from the moment he entered the stage.

The reader lacks 'simultaneity', all those visual and auditive elements which accompany the words, such as the outward appearance of a character, his gestures and the way he moves, or the intonation of his voice.[10] Of course, many of these elements are not embedded in the text, but rather filled in by director and actors. However when they *are* present in the text, a commentator can help the first-time reader to see what he is reading. In *Hamlet* I.2, for instance, the prince wears black, but unless this is indicated at the beginning of the scene, the reader only detects this important detail after 77 lines. At v. 782 of Aeschylus' *Agamemnon* the king enters in a chariot. The text does not yield this information until v. 906, and the presence of a woman in the chariot is only revealed in v. 950. Without the help of a commentator the reader's visualization of the scene would be very inadequate. It is different, of course, in the case of modern plays, which are usually provided with the author's stage directions, but when no such indications are added to the text, the reader may be temporarily deprived of essential information. It is, therefore, not without reason that Roux stipulates in her *Introduction*: 'Il est très important de *voir* Penthée' (22). Though the text makes

---

10. See for example the book of Hogendoorn.

clear that Pentheus is a very young man, this fact may easily escape the reader, the more so since the most pathetic references to his youth are made when he is already dead: νέον ἶνιν (1174); νέος ὁ μόσχος (1185).

In addition to these lines, Roux also draws attention to vv. 274, 330 and 974. However, v. 330 is irrelevant, since Cadmus calling his grandson ὦ παῖ is no indication of his age. Pheres, for instance, addresses his son in the same way (*Alcestis* 675), while Heracles is called τέκνον by Amphitryon (*Heracles* 610). On the other hand, the fact that the grandfather is still alive may have guided the expectation of the Athenian audience. We cannot deduce from the prologue (vv. 43-4) whether Cadmus is still alive. But from the moment this is clear (v. 170), the spectators were probably prepared for the appearance of a youth.

In v. 274 Tiresias, at the start of his pedantic exposé, addresses Pentheus with ὦ νεανία. This signal is ignored by Dodds, who is engrossed in the remarkable contents of Tiresias' forthcoming speech. Roux, on the other hand, does take note of Tiresias' form of address: 'ὦ νεανία: réplique à τὸ γῆρας (252); l'apostrophe insinue sans ménagement pour l'amour-propre de l'intéressé que ses opinions ne reposent que sur l'étourderie de la jeunesse. De plus, Tirésias semble s'excuser de formuler une vérité d'évidence qu'il serait inutile de rappeler à un esprit sérieux'. This amusing comment brings into focus Tiresias' attitude toward Pentheus; the form of address is seen as a means of characterizing the speaker. However, Roux discusses v. 971-6 from another angle: 'Le poète nous rappelle que ce dernier est un νεανίας: c'est à la fois une circonstance atténuante, comme le note Dodds (citant D.W. Lucas), et un moyen d'accroître la compassion des spectateurs pour le coupable'. Here Roux, like Dodds, only comments on the communication between poet and spectators, regardless of who is speaking. But why did the poet have to remind them of something they had been seeing throughout the play? Because in this scene Pentheus is in the guise of a woman? I think there is another question that needs to be answered: why does Euripides have *Dionysus* use the word νεανίας?

In his human shape Dionysus is, like Pentheus, a young man. If he wants to play his part convincingly, he cannot call his contemporary a νεανίας. And indeed he does not, in the preceding part of the tragedy. In his playful account of the 'palace miracles' he uses only Pentheus' proper name. When Pentheus has entered the palace to put on female clothes, Dionysus calls him 'the man': 'women, the man makes his way into the net' (v. 848). By calling Pentheus a man the god suggests that he is a well-matched opponent, a suggestion that is quite acceptable to the women of the chorus, since they were hitherto convinced that Pentheus had the power and the means to harm them. To the audience, who know that Pentheus was powerless from the beginning, the word 'man', at this precise moment, may well sound derisive: Pentheus is less of a man than ever.

Finally we come to v. 974. Dionysus speaks here his very last lines before leaving for the Cithaeron. By saying 'I and Bromios' he still keeps up appearances, but nevertheless his part as a young man has been played out. The chorus will not

see him again, not, that is, in his human shape; Pentheus no
longer hears or understands him.[11] By calling Pentheus νεανίας he dissociates himself from the role he played hitherto
and begins to return to his divine status. The word emphasizes
his superior power and the powerlessness of his victim. Thus
it may help to stir compassion, but not, I think, quite in the
way suggested by Roux.

In the present chapter I have tried to argue that 'the' spectators or 'the' audience are often the fruit of a scholar's imagi-
nation or the result of his personal interpretation. It is nearly
impossible to assess whether spectators forget what they know
or, in a body, start sympathizing with Pentheus during the
closing scenes of the *Bacchae* and not at an earlier stage of
the play. When presented as objective truths, such statements
are deceptive. The first is little more than a guess, the second
a kind of metaphor, standing for the author's interpretation.
Pronouncements on the Athenian audience are as a rule better
substantiated, but the evidence is often ambiguous. It must,
therefore, be weighed very carefully.

We have dealt here not with the knowledge of the audience, as in the previous chapters, but rather with their
thoughts and emotions. In general, scholars have not hesitated
to pronounce on these thoughts and emotions, while tending to
neglect what the audience knew and saw.

---

11.   It depends on the staging. If Dionysus addresses his final lines to his
victim's retreating back, Pentheus does not hear him. If the god speaks
while Pentheus is still near him, he does not understand him.

EPILOGUE

In the foregoing chapters I have explored the implications of the - obvious - fact that Greek tragedy was intended for spectators. And although I have listed a number of conclusions at the end of each chapter, it is perhaps appropriate to conclude this study with a brief survey of the main subjects discussed.

I agree with Dawson when he says: 'Any dispute as to the meaning and interpretation of a play takes us back to the words' (2). The meaning of a Greek tragedy is in its text. There is no sense in asking how much of this meaning was actually grasped by the original audience. The question cannot be answered and we cannot, moreover, speak of 'the' original audience in this connection, since its members must have differed considerably in such aspects as sensitivity, intellectual training, and memory. However, they had one thing in common: the plot of the play was new to all of them and revealed itself only gradually to their ears and eyes. This is a crucial fact, which we must take into account. When explaining the text we should be ever alert to the question: 'what did the audience know at this stage of the action?' If an interpretation is based on information not yet available to them and thus cannot have occurred to them, it is in principle not valid. In any case, it calls up questions which demand an answer. How did the audience explain what they heard? *Could* they explain it? And if they could not, what was the point in presenting them with a riddle, and when and how was the riddle solved?

In a number of cases the information available to the spectators was drawn from knowledge of the myth a play was based on. It is not always easy to reconstruct this knowledge, but the plays themselves are often of help. When the text contains information that is incomprehensible to an unknowing listener, we may safely assume that the poet was appealing to the prior knowledge of the audience, and expected them to understand what he meant. Thus it is possible to deduce from *Antigone* that the myth of Oedipus and his sons - though not the story of his daughters - was well-known at the time Sophocles wrote his play. And there is no reason to assume that this knowledge had disappeared by the time he created his *Oedipus Tyrannus*.

When a play was based on an well-known myth, the spectators knew the outcome of the tragedy but not how this outcome would be brought about. When a play was not based on such a myth they knew even less. It should be remembered that many a tragedy was built on a story that scarcely existed in any definite form. A tragedian might, for example, step in where myth ended. Aeschylus, like Stesichorus before him, asked: what happened to Orestes afterwards? and answered the question in a manner all his own. When Euripides, in turn, wrote his *Iphigenia in Tauris*, he was continuing where Aeschylus had left off. In the course of time the contents of such a play sometimes acquired the status of a mythical story. Thus I suppose that to many present-day people the plot of Sophocles' *Antigone* represents 'the' story of Antigone. In modern dramatic versions, however widely they may differ, the heroine always meets death after burying her brother. This apparently has become a fixed element of the story, an element that cannot be altered. However, this was not the case in antiquity. Euripides made Antigone live on to marry Haemon and to give birth to his son.

In attempting to assess what the audience knew, we must take into account their foreknowledge, that is, their knowledge of the unvarying elements of a myth: Oedipus killed his father and married his mother, Agamemnon was murdered at his homecoming, and so on. These are elements which no tragedian could alter without entering the realm of comedy[1], but furthermore he was free to develop his plot as he wanted. Thus a myth can never be equated with the contents of a poem or drama and prior knowledge of myth should not be confused with knowledge of a poetic or dramatic version of the same mythical material. Moreover, it is unlikely that such knowledge was ever shared by an audience as a whole. Where dramatic versions are concerned, the age of the spectator was an important factor; the older he was, the more tragedies he had seen. In the case of Aeschylus there might have been a recent restaging and a revival of work of other tragedians might have been seen by part of the spectators at a rural

---

1. Cf. Aristotle, *Poetics* 1453 a 35-39: in comedy Orestes and Aegisthus may make their exit as friends, but such things do not suit tragedy. The example may have been invented, but it is nevertheless illuminating.

festival. But generally speaking, a play that had been staged one or more decades earlier cannot have been known to all the members of an audience.

Sometimes a poet appealed to the audience's knowledge of an older play. It is generally assumed that this is what Euripides does in the recognition scene of his *Electra*. However, this is not the same as a poets's appeal to prior knowledge of myth, since the words of the characters in *Electra* are perfectly comprehensible to spectators who do not know the *Choephoroi*. Direct references such as this are rare, but knowledge of an earlier play may have influenced a spectator's response in a more general way, by stimulating his understanding. Thus when noting the differences between the play that lived in his memory and the play he was watching, he may well have become more keenly aware of the meaning of a line, a scene, or even the play as a whole. But of course the spectator's understanding never depended on his knowledge of an earlier drama. Each tragedy is an entity in its own right.

When discussing the dramatic impact of a line, a scene, or a choral ode, we should again ask ourselves: what did the audience know at this stage of the action? When Oedipus curses the murderer of Laius, there are two possibilities: either the audience knew that he is cursing himself or they did not and only realized in retrospect. These two possibilities entail two widely different ways of experiencing the scene. In this case the answer to our question seems clear: the audience *did* know. But where we are fairly sure that they did *not*, and shared the ignorance of the character or characters on stage, the term dramatic irony must not be used, since this would rob the term of its rightful meaning. There are, of course, instances where the question cannot be decided; when this is the case, the problem should at least been stated.

Even without superior knowledge an audience may have understood that a character was mistaken; they may have disagreed with his judgment and may have deemed him morally misguided long before he himself comes to this realization. In such cases, we could indeed use the term dramatic irony, but we should be aware of the difference between superior knowledge and superior judgment. The knowledge of the audience is, up to a point, verifiable, while their judgment is not. Dramatic irony based on superior judgment depends on our interpretation, on our conviction that the poet wanted his audience to see things in this particular way. And when we ascribe a judgment to them on the grounds of their world-view, the religious and political values they adhered to, and the opinions they shared, we should bear in mind that this world-view, and these values and opinions likewise depend on our interpretation and that here, too, interpretations may differ widely. The evidence should be carefully weighed; moreover we should bear in mind that the reality within a play cannot be equated with the reality outside.

As for the emotional reactions of the original audience, we can only speculate on the intensity of their involvement, their compassion and their fear, the more so since thousands of spectators cannot have reacted in exactly the same way. Statements on the emotions of 'the' audience, without further elaboration, simply do not make sense. Even the most intensive audience research can only reveal how part of a contemporary audience reacted to a specific performance, which itself reflects the interpretation of the man or woman who staged it. A pronouncement on the feelings of the audience is often a quasi-objective shorthand version of: 'according to my interpretation of the tragedy the poet wanted them to feel this way'. However, an observation like 'the audience are led to disbelieve what they know' may be quasi-objective, but it has nothing to do with one's interpretation. It is merely a guess, or at best a generalization, based on a reconstruction of the author's personal reaction. One may well wonder how reliable such a reconstruction can be.

I am aware that part of this study deals with the language we use when discussing Greek tragedy. However, words are the tools of our trade; we should know exactly what we mean by them.

APPENDIX

THE SOURCES CONCERNED WITH THE *PROAGON*

The *Vita Euripidis* recounts what happened at the *proagon* when the news of Euripides' death arrived. Sophocles appeared in mourning garment, actors and chorus came unwreathed and the audience burst into tears. This moving story does not add much to our knowledge of the proceedings, though there are two details not found in the other sources: the presence of the chorus and the wreathes. Apparently it was normal practice for chorus and actors to wear wreathes.

The scholium on *Wasps* explains the word Odeion: τόπος θεατροειδής, ἐν ᾧ εἰώθασι (or εἰώθεσαν according to the manuscript V) τὰ ποιήματα ἀπαγγέλλειν, πρὸ τῆς εἰς τὸ θέατρον ἀπαγγελίας. Pickard-Cambridge (67-8, n. 8) merely comments: 'The schol. on *Wasps* 1109 is probably not strictly correct in using the phrase τὰ ποιήματα ἀπαγγέλλειν, if the verb is used in the same sense as ἀπαγγελία in πρὸ τῆς εἰς τὸ θέατρον ἀπαγγελίας'. Unfortunately, he does not make clear what sense of ἀπαγγέλλειν or ἀπαγγελία he has in mind, but probably he thought of the meaning 'to recite' and 'recital'.[1] It is along these lines that Hiller explains the scholium. He supposes that, at the *proagon*, one play of each trilogy was recited and that in this way the poets tried to win the public's goodwill beforehand (403-4).

I find Hiller's theory untenable and slightly absurd. He himself points out that there was no music and no room for dancing. And there was clearly no stage-building either. The actors, without costumes or masks, mounted a kind of platform from which they faced the audience.[2] Now let us imagine for a moment such a recital of the *Oedipus Tyrannus*. At the end of the fourth epeisodion the protagonist, who recites the lines of Oedipus, cannot rush into the palace but has to wait quietly on his platform. The same applies to the actors who have just delivered the text of the herdsman and the messenger from Corinth. While they are waiting, the chorus sing - without benefit of music or dance - the fourth stasimon, whereupon the messenger takes over again. Of course, he is now no longer the messenger but the exangelos, but since the actor cannot change masks and cannot come out of the palace, this must be rather confusing. Perhaps the poet explained who was who? In any case, the exangelos reports what happened in the palace and concludes by announcing that the blind

---

1. Cf. the translation of Edmonds, I p. 703: 'The Odeum is a theatre-shaped building in which the works of poets are recited before being delivered on the stage'.

2. See Plato, *Symposium* 194 b: ἀναβαίνοντος ἐπὶ τὸν ὀκρίβαντα μετὰ τῶν ὑποκριτῶν.

Oedipus will soon come through the door. Unfortunately, he has to deliver his whole speech with Oedipus standing at his side. The effect of all this would be disconcerting if not devastating. Why on earth would a tragedian consent to exposing his plays to such a procedure? How could he warm up his future audience by presenting them with such a poor substitute for the real thing? And why would he rob the performance proper of every element of surprise?

Hiller's idea found little credence. If this is really what the scholiast meant, then he must have been mistaken. But is this even what he meant? The verb ἀπαγγέλλειν may mean 'to recite', though the meaning is rather unusual.[3] But the use of ἀπαγγελία to denote a theatrical performance would be very strange indeed. We need only think of Aristotle's observation that tragedy is a μίμησις ... δρώντων καὶ οὐ δι' ἀπαγγελίας (*Poetics* 1449 b 24-26). Moreover, why does the scholiast say ποιήματα instead of δράματα and why did he add the article? Strictly speaking τὰ ποιήματα would refer to all the plays, but did he not realize that a recital of nine tragedies and three satyr-plays on one day would be overdoing it?

It is quite possible that the scholiast misinterpreted his source or that his source itself was mistaken about the whole affair. But can we exclude the possibility that he is not referring to the *proagon* at all, but to some other ceremony now unknown to us? Or that he is using ἀπαγγέλλειν and ἀπαγγελία in another unusual sense? While I am unable to

---

3. LSJ, s.v. I,3 mention the meaning 'recite, declaim', but their only example is Choricius (*Rev.Phil* 1.220). Hiller (395 n. 2) has little to add: Synesius, *epist.* 111 and the *Suda* s.v. Καλλιφάνης and ῥαψῳδοί.

solve the problems presented by the scholium, I am quite convinced that it provides no information which is relevant to my discussion.

The same thing may be said of the scholium on Aeschines, though here there is no doubt that the scholiast is referring to the *proagon*. He describes it as follows: ἐγίγνοντο πρὸ τῶν μεγάλων Διονυσίων ἡμέραις ὀλίγαις ἔμπροσθεν ἐν τῷ Ὠιδείῳ καλουμένῳ τῶν τραγῳδῶν ἀγὼν καὶ ἐπίδειξις ὧν μέλλουσι δραμάτων ἀγωνίζεσθαι ἐν τῷ θεάτρῳ, δι' ὃ ἑτοίμως προαγὼν καλεῖται. εἰσίασι δὲ δίχα προσώπων οἱ ὑποκριταὶ γυμνοί. According to Pickard-Cambridge (67) he misunderstood the word: 'His "ἀγών" is probably a mistake, arising from his interpreting προαγών as "a preliminary contest", rather than as "a ceremony preliminary to the contest".' Though 'preliminary contest' seems the natural meaning of the word, Pickard-Cambridge is no doubt right that the *proagon* cannot have been a formal *agon*. We are then left with the substantive ἐπίδειξις, but the scholiast fails to explain *how* this ἐπίδειξις was given. Perhaps he did not know himself, or saw no reason to enter into details. After all, the reader need not know the ins and outs of the *proagon* to understand what Aeschines says.

Finally we come to Plato, who undoubtedly did know the details. But so did his readers, so that there was no need for him to explain things. To us, however, his words are somewhat ambiguous, as a closer inspection will show. Plato refers to the *proagon* (*Symposium* 194 a-b) in a short interlude between the speeches (λόγοι) of Aristophanes and Agathon. During this interlude Eryximachus remarks that it is good to know that both Agathon and Socrates (who will speak last) are experts on the subject of love, for otherwise they might be at a loss for words after such a variety of discourses. But Socrates still pretends to be nervous, and things will be even worse after Agathon has delivered his speech. Agathon, in turn, jokingly says he suspects that Socrates wants to confuse him by suggesting that the audience (τὸ θέατρον) expect him to speak exceedingly well. Socrates responds by reminding him of the *proagon*: even when facing so great an audience (τοσούτῳ θεάτρῳ) he was not confused, so he is not likely to be now. In his description of Agathon's courageous behaviour, there are only four words which may be relevant to our discussion: μέλλοντος ἐπιδείξεσθαι σαυτοῦ λόγους.

But are they relevant? Not according to Bury and Dover,[4] since both of them take the phrase as a reference to the performance of Agathon's plays at the festival proper and not to his announcement at the *proagon*. Bury comments: 'The force of μέλλοντος is seen when we remember that the ἀνάβασις of the poets took place at the προαγών, before the actual performance of the play...'. Now this is not quite true. The force of μέλλοντος cannot be understood without taking into account the tense of the infinitive, and it may be precisely the future tense of ἐπιδείξεσθαι which supports Bury's explanation. If the phrase were meant to indicate that Agathon was going to do or say something at the moment itself, then we would expect a present infinitive here.[5]

---

4. See their editions of Plato's *Symposium* and their comment ad loc.

5. See Ruijgh, 48-51.

Bury says nothing about the meaning of λόγους, but here Dover takes over: 'a dramatic poet can certainly be said to "display λόγοι of his own" in putting on a play'. One might add that the use of λόγος instead of δρᾶμα or τραγῳδία should be seen in the light of the context: by choosing this word Socrates connects the *proagon* with the symposion where Agathon is to deliver a λόγος, his speech about love.

If this interpretation is correct, then Plato's words do not help us to answer our initial question. And yet, since the future infinitive does not provide decisive proof, we cannot discard the explanation put forward by Pickard-Cambridge, who thinks that the Platonic phrase *does* refer to what Agathon said at the *proagon* itself. He infers from it that the poets informed the audience about the 'subjects of the plays' (67), adding in a note: 'As Haigh noted (*Att. Th.*, p. 68) λόγος is used of the subjects or plots in Ar. *Wasps* 54 and *Peace* 50, and in Hesych. s.v. λόγος· ἡ τοῦ δράματος ὑπόθεσις. It is also so used in the *Poetics* of Aristotle' (67-8 n. 8). However, if λόγος has the same meaning here, then the addition of σαυτοῦ is rather odd; one would rather expect σαυτοῦ τραγῳδιῶν λόγους. And even apart from σαυτοῦ, the parallels presented by Pickard-Cambridge do not establish the meaning of λόγος in Plato, as there is a considerable difference between λόγος in Aristophanes on the one hand, and in Aristotle and Hesychius on the other. As the slaves in Aristophanes' prologues are only human and cannot know what is going to happen, they do not explain the *plot* of the comedy, but merely the situation at the start of the play. Thus the only possible conclusion is that, even if the word λόγους denotes information about the plays and not the plays themselves, we are still none the wiser. *Mutatis mutandis* the poets may have provided the same kind of information as Aristophanes' slaves. As I concluded in chapter 2, I consider it highly improbable that they explained their plots. In any case, I hope that this appendix has shown that the sources give us very little to go on.

BIBLIOGRAPHY

The bibliography only contains books and articles that are mentioned in the text or the notes.

Aélion, Rachel   *Euripide Héritier d'Eschyle*, Tome 1 (Paris 1983)

Barrett, W.S.   *Euripides. Hippolytus* (Oxford 1964)

Beckerman, B.   *Dynamics of Drama. Theory and Method of Analysis* (New York 1970)

Behler, Ernst   *Klassische Ironie, romantische Ironie, tragische Ironie. Zum Ursprung dieser Begriffe* (Darmstadt 1972)

Bethe, E.   'Chrysippos', *RE* 3 (1899), 2498 2501

Biers, William R. &
     Thomas D. Boyd   'Ikarion in Attica: 1888-1981', *Hesperia* 51 (1982), 1-18

Blume, H.-D.   *Einführung in das antike Theaterwesen* (Darmstadt 1978)

Bond, G.W.   *Euripides. Heracles* (Oxford 1981)

Booth, Wayne C.   *The Rhetoric of Fiction* (Un. of Chicago Press 1961)

Bremer, J.M.   'Hoe bestudeert men een toneeltekst?', *Lampas* 4 (1971), 156-168

Bremer, J.M.   'Euripides *Heracles* 581', *CQ* 22 (1972), 236-240

Bulle, Heinrich   *Untersuchungen an griechischen Theatern* (München 1928)

Burton, R.W.B.   *The Chorus in Sophocles' Tragedies* (Oxford 1980)

Bury, R.G.   *The Symposium of Plato* (Cambridge 1932²)
Calder III, W.M.   'The Single-Performance Fallacy', *Educ. Theatre Journ.* 10 (1958), 237-239
Calder III, W.M.   'Sophokles' Political Tragedy, *Antigone*', *GRBS* 9 (1968), 389-407
Campbell, Lewis   *Sophocles. The Plays and Fragments, Vol. I* (Oxford 1879²; reprint Hildesheim 1969)
Chancellor, Gary   'Implicit Stage Directions in Ancient Greek Drama: Critical Assumptions and the Reading Public', *Arethusa* 12 (1979), 133-152
Collard, Christopher   *Euripides. Supplices* (Groningen 1975)
Conacher, D.J.   *Euripides. Alcestis* (Warminster 1988)
Davies, Malcolm   *Epicorum Graecorum Fragmenta* (Göttingen 1988)
Dawson, S.W.   *Drama and the Dramatic* (London 1970)
Dilke, D.A.W.   'Details and Chronology of Greek Theatre Caveas', *ABSA* 45 (1950), 21-62
Dodds, E.R.   *Euripides. Bacchae* (Oxford 1944, 1960²)
Dover, Kenneth   *Plato. Symposium* (Cambridge 1980)
Easterling, P.E.   *Sophocles. Trachiniae* (Cambridge 1982)
Edmonds, J.M.   *The Fragments of Attic Comedy* (Leiden 1957-1961)
Else, G.F.   *Aristotle's Poetics: the Argument* (Harvard Un. Press 1957)
Erp Taalman Kip, A.M. van   'Aeschylus *Agamemnon* 153: ΝΕΙΚΕΩΝ ΤΕΚΤΟΝΑ ΣΥΜΦΥΤΟΝ', *Mnemosyne* 39 (1986), 74-81
Fraenkel, E.   *Aeschylus. Agamemnon* (Oxford 1950)
Fritz, K. von   'Haimons Liebe zu Antigone'. In: *Antike und moderne Tragödie* (Berlin 1962), 227-240
Furley, William D.   'Motivation in the Parodos of Aeschylus' Agamemnon', *CPh* 81 (1986), 109-121
Gagarin, M.   *Aeschylean Drama* (Un. of California Press 1976)
Gardiner, Cynthia P.   *The Sophoclean Chorus. A Study of Character and Function* (Un. of Iowa Press 1987)

Groeneboom, P.	*Aeschylus' Zeven tegen Thebe* (Groningen 1938)
Groningen, B.A. van	'ΕΚΔΟΣΙΣ', *Mnemosyne* 16 (1963), 1-17
Harvey, F.D.	'Literacy in the Athenian Democracy', *REG* 79 (1966), 585-635
Havelock, E.A.	'The Oral Composition of Greek Drama', *QUCC* NS 6 (1980), 61-113
Heath, Malcolm	*The Poetics of Greek Tragedy* (London 1987)
Henderson, Jeffrey	'Older Women in Attic Old Comedy', *TAPHA* 117 (1987), 105-129
Hiller, E.	'Die athenischen Odeen und der ΠΡΟΑ-ΓΩΝ', *Hermes* 7 (1873), 393-407
Hirsch Jr, E.D.	'Three Dimensions of Hermeneutics', *New Literary History* 3 (1972), 245-261
Hogendoorn, W.	*Lezen en zien spelen* (Leiden 1976)
Hug, Arnold	*Platons Symposion* (Leipzig 1876)
Hutchinson, G.O.	*Aeschylus. Septem contra Thebas* (Oxford 1985)
Jebb, Richard	*Sophocles. The Plays and Fragments. Part III. The Antigone* (Cambridge 1906)
Johnson, S.K.	'Some Aspects of Dramatic Irony in Sophoclean Tragedy', *CR* 42 (1928), 209-214
Kamerbeek, J.C.	'Unity and Meaning of Euripides' *Heracles*', *Mnemosyne* 19 (1966), 1-16
Kamerbeek, J.C.	*The Plays of Sophocles. Commentaries. Part III. The Antigone* (Leiden 1978)
Kamerbeek, J.C.	*The Plays of Sophocles. Commentaries. Part IV. The Oedipus Tyrannus* (Leiden 1967)
Kannicht, R. & B. Snell	*Tragicorum Graecorum Fragmenta*, Vol. 2 (Göttingen 1981)
Kells, J.H.	*Sophocles. Electra* (Cambridge 1973)
Kirk, G.S.	*The Bacchae of Euripides* (Cambridge 1979)
Kirkwood, G.M.	*A Study of Sophoclean Drama* (Cornell Un. Press 1958)
Kitto, H.D.F.	*Poiesis. Structure and Thought* (Un. of California Press 1966)
Knox, Bernard M.W.	*Oedipus at Thebes* (Yale Un. Press 1957)

Knox, Bernard M.W.	*The Heroic Temper. Studies in Sophoclean Tragedy* (Un. of California Press 1964)
Knox, Bernard M.W.	'Books and readers in the Greek world. From the beginnings to Alexandria'. In: *The Cambridge History of Classical Literature, I,* ed. by P.E. Easterling and B.M.W. Knox (Cambridge 1985), 1-15
Kock, Th.	*Comicorum Atticorum Fragmenta,* Vol. II (Leipzig 1884)
Lamer, H.	'Laios', *RE* 12 (1925), 467-513
Lattimore, Richmond	*Story Patterns in Greek Tragedy* (London 1964)
Lebeck, Anne	*The Oresteia. A Study in Language and Structure* (Cambridge Mass. 1971)
Lee, K.H.	*Euripides. Troades* (London 1976)
Lefkowitz, Mary R.	*The Lives of the Greek Poets* (Johns Hopkins Un. Press 1981)
Lloyd-Jones, H.	'The Guilt of Agamemnon', *CQ* 12 (1962), 187-199
Lloyd-Jones, H.	*The Justice of Zeus* (Un. of California Press 1971, second ed. 1984)
Lucas, D.W.	*Aristotle. Poetics* (Oxford 1968)
Markantonatos, G.	''Tragic Irony' in the Antigone of Sophocles', *Emerita* 41 (1973), 491-497
Markantonatos, G.	*Studies in the History of the Concept of Eironeia and its Use as 'Tragic Irony' in Aeschylus, Sophocles and Euripides* (Un. of Southampton 1975)
Mathiessen, Kjeld	*Elektra, Taurische Iphigenie und Helena. Untersuchungen zur Chronologie und zur dramatischen Form im Spätwerk des Euripides* (Göttingen 1964)
Merkelbach, R. & M.L. West	*Fragmenta Hesiodea* (Oxford 1967)
Michelini, Ann Norris	*Euripides and the Tragic Tradition* (Un. of Wisconsin Press 1987)
Moles, J.	'Notes on Aristotle, *Poetics* 13 and 14', *CQ* 29 (1979), 77-94

Muecke, D.C.	*Irony* (London 1970)
Müller, G.	*Sophokles. Antigone* (Heidelberg 1967)
Oudemans, Th.C.W. & A.P.M.H. Lardinois	*Tragic Ambiguity: Anthropology, Philosophy and Sophocles' Antigone* (Leiden 1987)
Page, D.L.	*Poetae Melici Graeci* (Oxford 1962)
Petersmann, Hubert	'Mythos und Gestaltung in Sophokles' Antigone', *WS* 12 (1978), 67-96
Pfister, M.	*Das Drama. Theorie und Analyse* (München 1977)
Pickard-Cambridge, A.	*The Dramatic Festivals of Athens* (Oxford 1968², 1988³, revised by John Gould and D.M. Lewis)
Platnauer, M.	*Euripides. Iphigenia in Tauris* (Oxford 1938)
Podlecki, A.J.	'Reconstructing an Aeschylean Trilogy', *BICS* 22 (1975), 1-19
Pütz, P.	*Die Zeit im Drama. Zur Technik dramatischer Spannung* (Göttingen 1970)
Radt, Stefan	*Tragicorum Graecorum Fragmenta*, Vol. 4 (Göttingen 1977)
Rennie, W.	*The Acharnians of Aristophanes* (London 1909)
Rösler, W.	*Polis und Tragödie. Funktionsgeschichtliche Betrachtungen zu einer antiken Literaturgattung* (Konstanz 1980)
Romilly, Jacqueline de	*Time in Greek Tragedy* (Ithaca, N.Y. 1968)
Rosenmeyer, Thomas G.	'Irony and Tragic Choruses'. In: John H. D'Arms and John W. Eadie (eds.), *Ancient and Modern: Essays in Honor of Gerard F. Else* (Ann Arbor 1977), 31-44
Roux, Jeanne	*Euripide. Les Bacchantes* (Paris 1970)
Ruijgh, C.J.	'L'Emploi 'inceptif' du thème du présent du verbe grec', *Mnemosyne* 38 (1985), 1-61
Saïd, Suzanne	'Euripide ou l'attente déçue: l'exemple des Phéniciennes', *ASNP* 15 (1985), 501-527
Sedgewick, G.G.	*Of Irony: Especially in Drama* (Un. of Toronto Press 1935)

Sedgwick, W.B. — 'The Frogs and the Audience', *C. & M.* 9 (1947), 1-9

Sharpe, Robert Boies — *Irony in the Drama. An Essay on Impersonation, Shock and Catharsis* (Un. of North Carolina Press 1959)

Sicking, C.M.J. — *Aristophanes' Ranae. Een hoofdstuk uit de geschiedenis der Griekse Poëtica* (Assen 1962)

Smith, Peter M. — *On the Hymn to Zeus in Aeschylus' Agamemnon* (Am. Class. Studies 5, 1980)

Sommerstein, A.H. — 'Aristophanes and the Demon Poverty', *CQ* 34 (1984), 314-333

Stanford, W.B. — *Ambiguity in Greek Literature* (Oxford 1939)

Stanford, W.B. — *Aristophanes. The Frogs* (Oxford 1963²)

Stanford, W.B. — *Enemies of Poetry* (London 1980)

Stanford, W.B. — *Greek Tragedy and the Emotions. An introductory study* (London 1983)

Stanley, Audrey Eunice — *Early theatre structures in ancient Greece: a survey of archaeological and literary records from the Minoan period to 388 B.C.* (Ann Arbor: Un. Microfilms 1978)

States, Bert O. — *Irony and Drama. A Poetics* (Cornell Un. Press 1971)

Stevens, P.T. — 'Euripides and the Athenians', *JHS* 76 (1956), 87-94

Szlezák, Thomas Alexander — 'Sophokles' Elektra und das Problem des ironischen Dramas', *MH* 38 (1981), 1-21

Taplin, Oliver — *The Stagecraft of Aeschylus. The Dramatic Use of Exits and Entrances in Greek Tragedy* (Oxford 1977)

Taplin, Oliver — 'Did Greek dramatists write stage instructions?' *PCPhS* 23 (1977), 121-132

Thirlwall, C. — 'On the Irony of Sophocles', *The Phil. Museum* 2 (1833), 483-537

Turner, E.G. — *Athenian Books in the fifth and fourth centuries B.C.* (London 1952, 1977²)

Vellacott, Philip — *Ironic Drama. A Study of Euripides' Method and Meaning* (Cambridge 1975)

Veltruský, Jiří   *Drama as Literature* (Lisse 1977)

Virgilio, Rafaele di   'L'ironia tragica nell' 'Antigone' di Sofocle', *RFIC* 94 (1966), 26-33

Webster, T.B.L.   *An Introduction to Sophocles* (Oxford 1936, London 1969²)

Whitehead, David   *The Demes of Attica 508/7 - ca. 250 B.C. A Political and Social Study* (Princeton Un. Press 1986)

Wilamowitz-Moellendorff, Ulrich von   *Euripides. Herakles.* Erster Band: *Einleitung in die griechische Tragödie*; Zweiter Band (Darmstadt 1969)

Winnington-Ingram, R.P.   'Euripides: Poiêtes Sophos', *Arethusa* 2 (1969), 127-142

Winnington-Ingram, R.P.   *Sophocles. An Interpretation* (Cambridge 1980)

Woodbury, L.   'Aristophanes' Frogs and Athenian Literacy: Ran. 52-53, 1114', *TAPHA* 106 (1976), 349-357

GENERAL INDEX